Study Guide 1

Part One—Identifying Accounting Terms

Directions: Select the one term in Column I that best fits each definition in Column II. Print the letter identifying your choice in the Answers column.

Column I	Column II	Answers
A. account	1. Planning, recording, analyzing, and interpreting financial information. (p. 4)	1. _____
B. account balance	2. A planned process for providing financial information that will be useful to management. (p. 4)	2. _____
C. account title	3. Organized summaries of a business's financial activities. (p. 4)	3. _____
D. accounting	4. A business that performs an activity for a fee. (p. 6)	4. _____
E. accounting equation	5. A business owned by one person. (p. 6)	5. _____
F. accounting records	6. Anything of value that is owned. (p. 7)	6. _____
G. accounting system	7. Financial rights to the assets of a business. (p. 7)	7. _____
H. asset	8. An amount owed by a business. (p. 7)	8. _____
I. balance sheet	9. The amount remaining after the value of all liabilities is subtracted from the value of all assets. (p. 7)	9. _____
J. capital	10. An equation showing the relationship among assets, liabilities, and owner's equity. (p. 7)	10. _____
K. equities	11. A business activity that changes assets, liabilities, or owner's equity. (p. 9)	11. _____
L. liability	12. A record summarizing all the information pertaining to a single item in the accounting equation. (p. 9)	12. _____
M. owner's equity	13. The name given to an account. (p. 9)	13. _____
N. proprietorship	14. The amount in an account. (p. 9)	14. _____
O. service business	15. The account used to summarize the owner's equity in a business. (p. 9)	15. _____
P. transaction	16. A financial statement that reports assets, liabilities, and owner's equity on a specific date. (p. 13)	16. _____

Part Two—Identifying Accounting Concepts and Practices

Directions: Place a *T* for True or an *F* for False in the Answers column to show whether each of the following statements is true or false.

		Answers
1.	Accounting is the language of business. (p. 4)	1. ____
2.	Keeping personal and business records separate is an application of the business entity concept. (p. 6)	2. ____
3.	Assets such as cash and supplies have value because they can be used to acquire other assets or be used to operate a business. (p. 7)	3. ____
4.	The relationship among assets, liabilities, and owner's equity can be written as an equation. (p. 7)	4. ____
5.	The equation is called the accounting equation and does not have to be in balance to be correct. (p. 7)	5. ____
6.	The sum of the assets and liabilities of a business always equals the investment of the business owner. (p. 7)	6. ____
7.	Recording business costs in terms of hours required to complete projects and sales in terms of dollars is an application of the unit of measurement concept. (p. 9)	7. ____
8.	The capital account is an owner's equity account. (p. 9)	8. ____
9.	If two amounts are recorded on the same side of the accounting equation, the equation will no longer be in balance. (p. 10)	9. ____
10.	When a company pays insurance premiums in advance to an insurer, it records the payment as a liability because the insurer owes future coverage. (p. 10)	10. ____
11.	When items are bought and paid for later this is referred to as buying *on account*. (p. 11)	11. ____
12.	When cash is paid on account, a liability is increased. (p. 11)	12. ____
13.	The Going Concern accounting concept affects the way financial statements are prepared. (p. 13)	13. ____
14.	On a balance sheet, a single line means that amounts are to be added or subtracted. (p. 14)	14. ____

Part Three—Analyzing How Transactions Change an Accounting Equation

Directions: For each of the following transactions, select the two accounts in the accounting equation that are changed. Decide if each account is increased or decreased. Place a "+" in the column if the account is increased. Place a "−" in the column if the account is decreased.

Transactions
1–2. Received cash from owner as an investment. (p. 9)
3–4. Paid cash for supplies. (p. 10)
5–6. Paid cash for insurance. (p. 10)
7–8. Bought supplies on account from Ling Music Supplies. (p. 11)
9–10. Paid cash on account to Ling Music Supplies. (p. 11)

Trans. No.	Assets			=	Liabilities	+	Owner's Equity
	Cash	+ Supplies	+ Prepaid Insurance	=	Accts. Pay.—Ling Music Supplies	+	B. Treviño, Capital
1–2.							
3–4.							
5–6.							
7–8.							
9–10.							

Part Four—Analyzing a Balance Sheet

Directions: The parts of the balance sheet below are identified with capital letters. For each of the following items, decide which part is being described. Print the letter identifying your choice in the Answers column.

Answers

1. The total amount of equity in the business. (p. 14)

2. The label Assets. (p. 14)

3. The total amount owned by the business. (p. 14)

4. The name of the business. (p. 14)

5. The Liabilities section. (p. 14)

6. The name and date of the report. (p. 14)

7. The Assets section. (p. 14)

8. The amount of owner's equity. (p. 14)

9. The label Owner's Equity. (p. 14)

10. The label Liabilities. (p. 14)

Answers

1. _____

2. _____

3. _____

4. _____

5. _____

6. _____

7. _____

8. _____

9. _____

10. _____

Study Guide 2

Name	Perfect Score	Your Score
Identifying Accounting Terms	4 Pts.	
Identifying Accounting Concepts and Practices	15 Pts.	
Analyzing How Transactions Change an Accounting Equation	12 Pts.	
Analyzing a Balance Sheet	9 Pts.	
Total	40 Pts.	

Part One—Identifying Accounting Terms

Directions: Select the one term in Column I that best fits each definition in Column II. Print the letter identifying your choice in the Answers column.

Column I	Column II	Answers
A. expense	1. An increase in owner's equity resulting from the operation of a business. (p. 26)	1. _____
B. revenue	2. A sale for which cash will be received at a later date. (p. 26)	2. _____
C. sale on account	3. A decrease in owner's equity resulting from the operation of a business. (p. 27)	3. _____
D. withdrawals	4. Assets taken out of a business for the owner's personal use. (p. 28)	4. _____

Part Two—Identifying Accounting Concepts and Practices Related to Changes That Affect Owner's Equity

Directions: Place a *T* for True or an *F* for False in the Answers column to show whether each of the following statements is true or false.

1. A transaction for the sale of goods or services results in an increase in owner's equity. (p. 26)

   1. _____

2. When cash is received for services performed, the asset account Cash is increased and the owner's equity account is decreased. (p. 26)

   2. _____

3. Accounts Receivable is a liability account. (p. 26)

   3. _____

4. Regardless of when payment is made when services are sold, the revenue should be recorded at the time of the sale. (p. 26)

   4. _____

5. A transaction that increases accounts receivable and increases owner's equity is a sale on account. (p. 26)

   5. _____

6. Owner's equity is decreased by a sale on account. (p. 26)

   6. _____

7. When cash is paid for expenses, the business has less cash; therefore, the asset account Cash is decreased and the owner's equity account is increased. (p. 27)

   7. _____

8. Cash is increased by expenses. (p. 27)

   8. _____

9. Recording an expense transaction in an accounting equation increases liabilities. (p. 27)

   9. _____

10. When a company makes payments for advertising and charitable contributions, the company is paying expenses. (p. 27)

    10. _____

11. When a company receives cash from a customer for a prior sale, the transaction decreases the cash account balance and increases the accounts receivable balance. (p. 28)

    11. _____

12. A withdrawal is a transaction that decreases cash and decreases owner's equity. (p. 28)

    12. _____

13. When cash is paid to the owner for personal use, assets decrease and owner's equity decreases. (p. 28)

    13. _____

14. An owner may withdraw only cash from a business; other assets must remain in the business at all times for the accounting equation to be in balance. (p. 28)

    14. _____

15. Three transactions that affect owner's equity are receiving cash on account, paying expenses, and paying for supplies bought on account. (p. 28)

    15. _____

Part Three—Analyzing How Transactions That Affect Owner's Equity Change an Accounting Equation

Directions: For each of the following transactions, select the two accounts in the accounting equation that are changed. Decide if each account is increased or decreased. Place a "+" in the column if the account is increased. Place a "−" in the column if the account is decreased.

Transactions

1–2. Received cash from sales. (p. 26)
3–4. Sold services on account to Kids Time. (p. 26)
5–6. Paid cash for rent. (p. 27)
7–8. Paid cash for telephone bill. (p. 27)
9–10. Received cash on account from Kids Time. (p. 28)
11–12. Paid cash to owner for personal use. (p. 28)

Trans. No.	Assets				=	Liabilities	+	Owner's Equity
	Cash	+	Accts. Rec.—Kids Time	+	Supplies	+	Prepaid Insurance	=	Accts. Pay.—Ling Music Supplies	+	B. Treviño, Capital
1–2.								
3–4.								
5–6.								
7–8.								
9–10.								
11–12.								

Part Four—Analyzing a Balance Sheet

Directions: Place a *T* for True or an *F* for False in the Answers column to show whether each of the following statements is true or false.

1. A balance sheet may be prepared on any date. (p. 30)

   1. _____

2. The accounts on the left side of the accounting equation are reported on the left side of the balance sheet. (p. 30)

   2. _____

3. Few businesses need to prepare a balance sheet every day. (p. 30)

   3. _____

4. The balance sheet reports the balances of the asset, liability, and owner's equity accounts. (p. 30)

   4. _____

5. The heading of a balance sheet contains the name of the business, name of the report, and date of the report. (p. 30)

   5. _____

6. The accounts on the left side of the accounting equation include the liabilities and owner's equity. (p. 30)

   6. _____

7. The total of the left side of the balance sheet is equal to the right side, and these totals need not be on the same line. (p. 30)

   7. _____

8. Asset accounts are shown on the right side of the balance sheet. (p. 30)

   8. _____

9. Owner's equity accounts are presented above liability accounts on the balance sheet. (p. 30)

   9. _____

Study Guide 3

Part One—Identifying Accounting Terms

Directions: Select the one term in Column I that best fits each definition in Column II. Print the letter identifying your choice in the Answers column.

Column I	Column II	Answers
A. chart of accounts	1. An accounting device used to analyze transactions. (p. 42)	1. _____
B. credit	2. The side of the account that is increased. (p. 42)	2. _____
C. debit	3. An amount recorded on the left side. (p. 42)	3. _____
D. normal balance	4. An amount recorded on the right side. (p. 42)	4. _____
E. T account	5. A list of accounts used by a business. (p. 45)	5. _____

Part Two—Analyzing Transactions into Debit and Credit Parts

Directions: Analyze each of the following transactions into debit and credit parts. Print the letter identifying your choice in the proper Answers columns.

Account Titles

A. Cash
B. Accounts Receivable—Kids Time
C. Supplies
D. Prepaid Insurance
E. Accounts Payable—Ling Music Supplies
F. Barbara Treviño, Capital
G. Barbara Treviño, Drawing
H. Sales
I. Rent Expense

	Answers	
	Debit	**Credit**
1–2. Received cash from owner as an investment. (p. 45)	1._____	2._____
3–4. Paid cash for supplies. (p. 46)	3._____	4._____
5–6. Paid cash for insurance. (p. 47)	5._____	6._____
7–8. Bought supplies on account from Ling Music Supplies. (p. 48)	7._____	8._____
9–10. Paid cash on account to Ling Music Supplies. (p. 49)	9._____	10._____
11–12. Received cash from sales. (p. 51)	11._____	12._____
13–14. Sold services on account to Kids Time. (p. 52)	13._____	14._____
15–16. Paid cash for rent. (p. 53)	15._____	16._____
17–18. Received cash on account from Kids Time. (p. 54)	17._____	18._____
19–20. Paid cash to owner for personal use. (p. 55)	19._____	20._____

Part Three—Identifying Changes in Accounts

Directions: For each of the following items, select the choice that best completes the statement. Print the letter identifying your choice in the Answers column.

Answers

1. The values of all things owned (assets) are on the account equation's (A) left side (B) right side (C) credit side (D) none of these. (p. 40)

   1. _____

2. The values of all equities or claims against the assets (liabilities and owner's equity) are on the account equation's (A) left side (B) right side (C) debit side (D) none of these. (p. 40)

   2. _____

3. An amount recorded on the left side of a T account is a (A) debit (B) credit (C) normal balance (D) none of these. (p. 42)

   3. _____

4. An amount recorded on the right side of a T account is a (A) debit (B) credit (C) normal balance (D) none of these. (p. 42)

   4. _____

5. The normal balance side of any asset account is the (A) debit side (B) credit side (C) right side (D) none of these. (p. 42)

   5. _____

6. The normal balance side of any liability account is the (A) debit side (B) credit side (C) left side (D) none of these. (p. 42)

   6. _____

7. The normal balance side of an owner's capital account is the (A) debit side (B) credit side (C) left side (D) none of these. (p. 42)

   7. _____

8. Debits must equal credits (A) in a T account (B) on the equation's left side (C) on the equation's right side (D) in all transactions. (p. 45)

   8. _____

9. Decreases in an asset account are shown on a T account's (A) debit side (B) credit side (C) balance side (D) none of these. (p. 45)

   9. _____

10. Decreases in any liability account are shown on a T account's (A) debit side (B) credit side (C) right side (D) none of these. (p. 49)

    10. _____

11. Increases in an owner's capital account are shown on a T account's (A) debit side (B) credit side (C) left side (D) none of these. (p. 51)

    11. _____

12. Increases in a revenue account are shown on a T account's (A) debit side (B) credit side (C) left side (D) none of these. (p. 51)

    12. _____

13. The normal balance side of any revenue account is the (A) debit side (B) credit side (C) left side (D) none of these. (p. 51)

    13. _____

14. The normal balance side of any expense account is the (A) debit side (B) credit side (C) right side (D) none of these. (p. 53)

    14. _____

15. The normal balance side of an owner's drawing account is the (A) debit side (B) credit side (C) left side (D) none of these. (p. 55)

    15. _____

Study Guide 4

Name		Perfect Score	Your Score
	Identifying Accounting Terms	13 Pts.	
	Identifying Accounting Concepts and Practices	17 Pts.	
	Analyzing a Five-Column Journal	10 Pts.	
	Recording Transactions in a Five-Column Journal	20 Pts.	
	Total	60 Pts.	

Part One—Identifying Accounting Terms

Directions: Select the one term in Column I that best fits each definition in Column II. Print the letter identifying your choice in the Answers column.

Column I	Column II	Answers
A. check	**1.** A form for recording transactions in chronological order. (p. 64)	1. _____
B. double-entry accounting	**2.** Recording transactions in a journal. (p. 64)	2. _____
C. entry	**3.** A journal amount column headed with an account title. (p. 66)	3. _____
D. general amount column	**4.** A journal amount column that is not headed with an account title. (p. 66)	4. _____
E. invoice	**5.** Information for each transaction recorded in a journal. (p. 66)	5. _____
F. journal	**6.** The recording of debit and credit parts of a transaction. (p. 66)	6. _____
G. journalizing	**7.** A business paper from which information is obtained for a journal entry. (p. 66)	7. _____
H. memorandum	**8.** A business form ordering a bank to pay cash from a bank account. (p. 67)	8. _____
I. proving cash	**9.** A form describing the goods or services sold, the quantity, and the price. (p. 67)	9. _____
J. receipt	**10.** An invoice used as a source document for recording a sale on account. (p. 67)	10. _____
K. sales invoice	**11.** A business form giving written acknowledgment for cash received. (p. 68)	11. _____
L. source document	**12.** A form on which a brief message is written describing a transaction. (p. 68)	12. _____
M. special amount column	**13.** Determining that the amount of cash agrees with the accounting records. (p. 85)	13. _____

Part Two—Identifying Accounting Concepts and Practices

Directions: Place a *T* for True or an *F* for False in the Answers column to show whether each of the following statements is true or false.

1. Transactions are recorded in a journal in order by date and in one place. (p. 66)   1. _____

2. The Objective Evidence accounting concept requires that there be proof that a transaction did occur. (p. 66)   2. _____

3. Examples of source documents include checks, sales invoices, memorandums, and letters. (p. 66)   3. _____

4. The source document for all cash payments is a sales invoice. (p. 67)   4. _____

5. A check is the source document used when items are paid in cash. (p. 67)   5. _____

6. A receipt is the source document for cash received from transactions other than sales. (p. 68)   6. _____

7. A calculator tape is the source document for daily sales. (p. 68)   7. _____

8. The source document used when supplies are bought on account is a memorandum. (p. 73)   8. _____

9. The source document used when supplies bought on account are paid for is a check. (p. 74)   9. _____

10. The journal columns used to record receiving cash from sales are cash debit and sales credit. (p. 76)   10. _____

11. The source document *sales invoice* is abbreviated as SI in a journal entry. (p. 77)   11. _____

12. The journal columns used to record paying cash for rent are general debit and cash credit. (p. 78)   12. _____

13. The journal columns used to record paying cash to the owner for personal use are general debit and cash credit. (p. 80)   13. _____

14. To prove a journal page, the total debit amounts are compared with the total credit amounts to be sure they are equal. (p. 82)   14. _____

15. Double lines across column totals mean that the totals have been verified as correct. (p. 85)   15. _____

16. To correct an error in a journal, simply erase the incorrect item and write the correct item in the same place. (p. 86)   16. _____

17. Dollars and cents signs and decimal points should be used when writing amounts on ruled accounting pages. (p. 86)   17. _____

Part Three—Analyzing a Five-Column Journal

Directions: The columns of the journal below are identified with capital letters. For each of the following items, decide which column is being described. Print the letter identifying your choice in the Answers column.

JOURNAL   PAGE

	DATE	ACCOUNT TITLE	DOC. NO.	POST. REF.	GENERAL DEBIT	GENERAL CREDIT	SALES CREDIT	CASH DEBIT	CASH CREDIT	
1	A	B	C	D	E	F	G	H	I	1
2										2
3										3

Answers

1. Write the year for the first entry on a journal page. (p. 69)

   1. _____

2. Write the name of the month for the first entry. (p. 69)

   2. _____

3. Write the account title for an amount in the General Credit column. (p. 69)

   3. _____

4. Write the credit amount when cash is received from the owner as an investment. (p. 69)

   4. _____

5. Write the source document number for an entry. (p. 69)

   5. _____

6. Write the account title for an amount in the General Debit column. (p. 70)

   6. _____

7. Write the amount credited to Sales. (p. 76)

   7. _____

8. Indicate with a check mark that no account title needs to be written for an entry. (p. 76)

   8. _____

9. Write the debit amount when cash is received from sales. (p. 76)

   9. _____

10. Write the amount debited to Rent Expense. (p. 78)

   10. _____

Part Four—Recording Transactions in a Five-Column Journal

Directions: Use the journal in Part Three. For each of the following transactions, decide which debit and credit amount columns will be used. Print the letters identifying your choice in the proper Answers columns.

		Answers	
		Debit	**Credit**
1–2.	Received cash from owner as an investment. (p. 69)	1. _____	2. _____
3–4.	Paid cash for supplies. (p. 70)	3. _____	4. _____
5–6.	Paid cash for insurance. (p. 72)	5. _____	6. _____
7–8.	Bought supplies on account. (p. 73)	7. _____	8. _____
9–10.	Paid cash on account. (p. 74)	9. _____	10. _____
11–12.	Received cash from sales. (p. 76)	11. _____	12. _____
13–14.	Sold services on account. (p. 77)	13. _____	14. _____
15–16.	Paid cash for an expense. (p. 78)	15. _____	16. _____
17–18.	Received cash on account. (p. 79)	17. _____	18. _____
19–20.	Paid cash to owner for personal use. (p. 80)	19. _____	20. _____

Name	Perfect Score	Your Score
Identifying Accounting Terms	7 Pts.	
Identifying Accounting Concepts and Practices	19 Pts.	
Identifying Accounting Concepts	11 Pts.	
Analyzing Posting from a Journal to a General Ledger	13 Pts.	
Total	50 Pts.	

Part One—Identifying Accounting Terms

Directions: Select the one term in Column I that best fits each definition in Column II. Print the letter identifying your choice in the Answers column.

Column I	Column II	Answers
A. account number	1. A group of accounts. (p. 99)	1. _____
B. correcting entry	2. A ledger that contains all accounts needed to prepare financial statements. (p. 99)	2. _____
C. file maintenance	3. The number assigned to an account. (p. 99)	3. _____
D. general ledger	4. The procedure for arranging accounts in a general ledger, assigning account numbers, and keeping records current. (p. 100)	4. _____
E. ledger	5. Writing an account title and number on the heading of an account. (p. 101)	5. _____
F. opening an account	6. Transferring information from a journal entry to a ledger account. (p. 103)	6. _____
G. posting	7. A journal entry made to correct an error in a ledger. (p. 116)	7. _____

Part Two—Identifying Accounting Concepts and Practices

Directions: Place a *T* for True or an *F* for False in the Answers column to show whether each of the following statements is true or false.

1. Because an account form has columns for the debit and credit balance of an account, it is often referred to as the balance-ruled account form. (p. 98)

   1. _____

2. The asset division accounts for Encore Music are numbered in the 100s. (p. 99)

   2. _____

3. The cash account is the first asset account and is numbered 100. (p. 99)

   3. _____

4. The second division of Encore Music's chart of accounts is the owner's equity division. (p. 99)

   4. _____

5. The first digit of account numbers for accounts in the owner's equity ledger division is 3. (p. 99)

   5. _____

6. The last two digits in a 3-digit account number indicate the general ledger division of the account. (p. 99)

   6. _____

7. When adding a new expense account between accounts numbered 510 and 520, the new account is assigned the account number 515. (p. 100)

   7. _____

8. Encore Music arranges expense accounts in chronological order in its general ledger. (p. 100)

   8. _____

9. The two steps for opening an account are writing the account title and recording the balance. (p. 101)

   9. _____

10. Separate amounts in special amount columns are posted individually. (p. 103)

    10. _____

11. Separate amounts in a Sales Credit column are not posted individually. (p. 103)

    11. _____

12. Separate amounts in general amount columns are not posted individually. (p. 103)

    12. _____

13. The posting reference should always be recorded in the journal's Post. Ref. column before amounts are recorded in the ledger. (p. 104)

    13. _____

14. The only reason for the Post. Ref. columns of the journal and general ledger is to indicate which entries in the journal still need to be posted if posting is interrupted. (p. 104)

    14. _____

15. The steps for posting are to write the date, journal page number, amount, and balance. (p. 105)

    15. _____

16. The totals of general amount columns in a journal are not posted. (p. 107)

    16. _____

17. The totals of special amount columns in a journal are not posted. (p. 108)

    17. _____

18. A check mark in parentheses below a General Debit column total indicates that the total is not posted. (p. 107)

    18. _____

19. With the exception of the totals lines, the Post Ref. Column is completely filled in with either an account number or a check mark. (p. 112)

    19. _____

Part Three—Identifying Accounting Concepts

Directions: Place a check mark in the proper Answers column to show whether each of the following statements is best described as a debit or a credit.

	Answers	
	Debit	**Credit**
1. Normal balance of Supplies. (p. 103)	_____	_____
2. Column in the accounts payable account in which an entry for supplies bought on account is posted. (p. 104)	_____	_____
3. Normal balance of owner's capital account. (p. 105)	_____	_____
4. Balance column in the capital account after an initial investment is posted. (p. 105)	_____	_____
5. Normal balance of Sales. (p. 108)	_____	_____
6. Account balance column in which the account balance is recorded when the only entry is a credit. (p. 108)	_____	_____
7. Normal balance of Cash. (p. 109)	_____	_____
8. Balance column in the cash account after the special amount column totals for Cash are posted. (p. 110)	_____	_____
9. Account balance column in which the account balance is recorded when the debit balance exceeds the credit entry. (p. 110)	_____	_____
10. Account balance column in which the new account balance is recorded when the previous balance is a debit of $500.00 and the current entry is a credit of $200.00. (p. 110)	_____	_____
11. Normal balance of Rent Expense. (p. 115)	_____	_____

Part Four—Analyzing Posting from a Journal to a General Ledger

Directions: In the journal below, some items are identified with capital letters. In the general ledger accounts, locations to which items are posted are identified with numbers. For each number in a general ledger account, select the letter in the journal that will be posted to the account. Print the letter identifying your choice in the Answers column.

JOURNAL PAGE 1 A

	DATE		ACCOUNT TITLE	DOC. NO.	POST. REF.	GENERAL DEBIT	GENERAL CREDIT	SALES CREDIT	CASH DEBIT	CASH CREDIT	
1	20-- May	2	Adam Oliver, Capital	R1		1 0 0 0 00				1 0 0 0 00	1
2		4	Supplies	C1		2 0 0 00 ←B				2 0 0 00	2
3		6	✓	T6	✓			8 0 0 00 ←C		8 0 0 00	3
25		31	Totals			2 0 5 5 00	5 0 0 00	3 4 0 0 00	3 9 0 0 00	2 0 5 5 00	25
26	D	E		F		G	H	I	J	K	26

ACCOUNT Cash   ACCOUNT NO. 110

DATE		ITEM	POST. REF.	DEBIT	CREDIT	BALANCE DEBIT	BALANCE CREDIT
1	2		3	4			
					5		

ACCOUNT Supplies   ACCOUNT NO. 120

DATE		ITEM	POST. REF.	DEBIT	CREDIT	BALANCE DEBIT	BALANCE CREDIT
6	7		8	9			

ACCOUNT Sales   ACCOUNT NO. 410

DATE		ITEM	POST. REF.	DEBIT	CREDIT	BALANCE DEBIT	BALANCE CREDIT
10	11		12		13		

A through F (pp. 103–105)

G through K (pp. 107–110)

Bold Numbers in Ledger Accounts   **Answers**

1. _____ _____

2. _____ _____

3. _____ _____

4. _____ _____

5. _____ _____

6. _____ _____

7. _____ _____

8. _____ _____

9. _____ _____

10. _____ _____

11. _____ _____

12. _____ _____

13. _____ _____

Study Guide 6

Part One—Identifying Accounting Terms

Directions: Select the one term in Column I that best fits each definition in Column II. Print the letter identifying your choice in the Answers column.

Column I	Column II	Answers
A. bank statement	**1.** A bank account from which payments can be ordered by a depositor. (p. 126)	1._____
B. blank endorsement	**2.** A signature or stamp on the back of a check, transferring ownership. (p. 127)	2._____
C. checking account	**3.** An endorsement consisting only of the endorser's signature. (p. 127)	3._____
D. debit card	**4.** An endorsement indicating a new owner of a check. (p. 127)	4._____
E. dishonored check	**5.** An endorsement restricting further transfer of a check's ownership. (p. 127)	5._____
F. electronic funds transfer	**6.** A check with a future date on it. (p. 128)	6._____
G. endorsement	**7.** A report of deposits, withdrawals, and bank balances sent to a depositor by a bank. (p. 131)	7._____
H. petty cash	**8.** A check that a bank refuses to pay. (p. 136)	8._____
I. petty cash slip	**9.** A computerized cash payments system that uses electronic impulses to transfer funds. (p. 138)	9._____
J. postdated check	**10.** A bank card that, when making purchases, automatically deducts the amount of the purchase from the checking account of the cardholder. (p. 139)	10._____
K. restrictive endorsement	**11.** An amount of cash kept on hand and used for making small payments. (p. 141)	11._____
L. special endorsement	**12.** A form showing proof of a petty cash payment. (p. 142)	12._____

Part Two—Analyzing Transactions in a Cash Control System

Directions: Analyze each of the following transactions into debit and credit parts. Print the letters identifying your choices in the proper Answers columns.

Account Titles

A. Cash
B. Petty Cash
C. Accounts Receivable—B. Johnson

D. Supplies
E. Accounts Payable—Super Supplies
F. Miscellaneous Expense

Transactions		Answers	
		Debit	Credit
1–2.	Received bank statement showing bank service charge. (p. 134)	1. _____	2. _____
3–4.	Received notice from a bank of a dishonored check from B. Johnson. (p. 137)	3. _____	4. _____
5–6.	Paid cash on account to Super Supplies using EFT. (p. 138)	5. _____	6. _____
7–8.	Purchased supplies using a debit card. (p. 139)	7. _____	8. _____
9–10.	Paid cash to establish a petty cash fund. (p. 141)	9. _____	10. _____
11–12.	Paid cash to replenish a petty cash fund: $12.00, supplies; $3.50, miscellaneous expense. (p. 143)	11. _____	12. _____

Part Three—Identifying Accounting Concepts and Practices

Directions: Place a *T* for True or an *F* for False in the Answers column to show whether each of the following statements is true or false.

Answers

1. Because cash transactions occur more frequently than other transactions, the chances for making recording errors affecting cash are less. (p. 124)

1. _____

2. When a deposit is made in a bank account, the bank issues a receipt. (p. 126)

2. _____

3. There are four types of endorsements commonly used: blank, special, original, and restrictive. (p. 127)

3. _____

4. A check with a blank endorsement can be cashed by anyone who has the check. (p. 127)

4. _____

5. When writing a check, the first step is to prepare the check stub. (p. 128)

5. _____

6. Most banks do not look at the date the check is written and will withdraw money from the depositor's account anytime. (p. 128)

6. _____

7. The amount of a check is written twice on each check. (p. 128)

7. _____

8. A check that contains errors must be marked with the word VOID and another check must be written. (p. 129)

8. _____

9. An outstanding check is one that has been issued but not yet reported on a bank statement by the bank. (p. 131)

9. _____

10. An important aspect of cash control is verifying that the information on a bank statement and a checkbook are in agreement. (p. 132)

10. _____

11. Banks deduct service charges from customers' checking accounts without requiring customers to write a check for the amount. (p. 133)

11. _____

12. Not only do banks charge a fee for handling a dishonored check, but they also deduct the amount of the check from the account as well. (p. 136)

12. _____

13. The journal entry for a payment on account using electronic funds transfer is exactly the same as when the payment is made by check. (p. 138)

13. _____

14. The source document for an electronic funds transfer is a memorandum. (p. 138)

14. _____

15. The source document for a debit card purchase is a memorandum. (p. 139)

15. _____

16. Encore Music maintains a petty cash fund for making large cash payments without writing checks. (p. 141)

16. _____

17. Using a petty cash fund usually decreases the number of checks that have to be written. (p. 141)

17. _____

18. A memorandum is the source document for the entry to record establishing a petty cash fund. (p. 141)

18. _____

19. Anytime a payment is made from the petty cash fund, a petty cash slip is prepared showing proof of a petty cash payment. (p. 142)

19. _____

20. When the petty cash fund is replenished, the balance of the petty cash account increases. (p. 143)

20. _____

Study Guide 7

Name		Perfect Score	Your Score
	Identifying Accounting Terms	7 Pts.	
	Analyzing Accounting Practices Related to a Work Sheet	17 Pts.	
	Analyzing the Preparation of a Trial Balance on a Work Sheet	16 Pts.	
	Analyzing Adjustments and Extending Account Balances on a Work Sheet	16 Pts.	
	Total	56 Pts.	

Part One—Identifying Accounting Terms

Directions: Select the one term in Column I that best fits each definition in Column II. Print the letter identifying your choice in the Answers column.

Column I	Column II	Answers
A. adjustments	**1.** The length of time for which a business summarizes and reports financial information. (p. 156)	1. _____
B. fiscal period	**2.** A columnar accounting form used to summarize the general ledger information needed to prepare financial statements. (p. 156)	2. _____
C. income statement	**3.** A proof of the equality of debits and credits in a general ledger. (p. 157)	3. _____
D. net income	**4.** Changes recorded on a work sheet to update general ledger accounts at the end of a fiscal period. (p. 160)	4. _____
E. net loss	**5.** A financial statement showing the revenue and expenses for a fiscal period. (p. 166)	5. _____
F. trial balance	**6.** The difference between total revenue and total expenses when total revenue is greater. (p. 167)	6. _____
G. work sheet	**7.** The difference between total revenue and total expenses when total expenses is greater. (p. 168)	7. _____

Part Two—Analyzing Accounting Practices Related to a Work Sheet

Directions: Place a *T* for True or an *F* for False in the Answers column to show whether each of the following statements is true or false.

Answers

1. The accounting concept Consistent Reporting is being applied when a word processing service business reports revenue per page one year and revenue per hour the next year. (p. 154)

1. _____

2. An accounting period is also known as a fiscal period. (p. 156)

2. _____

3. Journals, ledgers, and work sheets are considered permanent records. (p. 156)

3. _____

4. All general ledger account titles are listed on a trial balance in the same order as listed on the chart of accounts. (p. 157)

4. _____

5. The four questions asked when analyzing an adjustment are: Why? Where? When? and How? (p. 161)

5. _____

6. The two accounts affected by the adjustment for supplies are Supplies and Supplies Expense. (p. 161)

6. _____

7. The two accounts affected by the adjustment for insurance are Prepaid Insurance Expense and Insurance. (p. 162)

7. _____

8. Totaling and ruling the Adjustments columns of a work sheet is necessary to prove the equality of debits and credits. (p. 163)

8. _____

9. Two financial statements are prepared from the information on the work sheet. (p. 165)

9. _____

10. Net income on a work sheet is calculated by subtracting the Income Statement Credit column total from the Income Statement Debit column total. (p. 167)

10. _____

11. If errors are found on a work sheet, they must be erased and corrected before any further work is completed. (p. 170)

11. _____

12. When two column totals are not in balance on the work sheet, the difference between the two totals is calculated and checked. (p. 170)

12. _____

13. If the difference between the totals of Debit and Credit columns on a work sheet can be evenly divided by 9, then the error is most likely in addition. (p. 170)

13. _____

14. If there are errors in the work sheet's Trial Balance columns, it might be because not all general ledger account balances were copied in the Trial Balance column correctly. (p. 171)

14. _____

15. Errors in general ledger accounts should never be erased. (p. 172)

15. _____

16. Most errors occur in doing arithmetic. (p. 172)

16. _____

17. Using a calculator will help prevent errors in accounting records, but not all errors are due to incorrect calculations. (p. 173)

17. _____

Part Three—Analyzing the Preparation of a Trial Balance on a Work Sheet

Directions: For each account title listed below, decide whether the account balance is recorded in the Trial Balance Debit or Trial Balance Credit column. Place a check mark in the proper Answers column identifying your choice. (p. 157)

	Trial Balance Debit	Credit
1. Cash	____	____
2. Petty Cash	____	____
3. Accounts Receivable—Lawrence Roofing	____	____
4. Supplies	____	____
5. Prepaid Insurance	____	____
6. Accounts Payable—Simpson's Supplies	____	____
7. Sophia Cruse, Capital	____	____
8. Sophia Cruse, Drawing	____	____
9. Income Summary	____	____
10. Sales	____	____
11. Advertising Expense	____	____
12. Insurance Expense	____	____
13. Miscellaneous Expense	____	____
14. Rent Expense	____	____
15. Supplies Expense	____	____
16. Utilities Expense	____	____

Part Four—Analyzing Adjustments and Extending Account Balances on a Work Sheet

Directions: For each account listed below, determine in which work sheet column(s) an amount typically will be written. Place a check mark in the proper Answers column to show your answer.

	Adjustments Debit Credit (pp. 161–162)		Income Statement Debit Credit (p. 166)		Balance Sheet Debit Credit (p. 165)	
1. Cash						
2. Petty Cash						
3. Accounts Receivable—Lawrence Roofing						
4. Supplies						
5. Prepaid Insurance						
6. Accounts Payable—Simpson's Supplies						
7. Sophia Cruse, Capital						
8. Sophia Cruse, Drawing						
9. Income Summary						
10. Sales						
11. Advertising Expense						
12. Insurance Expense						
13. Miscellaneous Expense						
14. Rent Expense						
15. Supplies Expense						
16. Utilities Expense						

Study Guide 8

Name		Perfect Score	Your Score
Identifying Accounting Concepts and Practices		20 Pts.	
Analyzing an Income Statement		15 Pts.	
Analyzing Income Statement Procedures		5 Pts.	
	Total	40 Pts.	

Part One—Identifying Accounting Concepts and Practices

Directions: Place a *T* for True or an *F* for False in the Answers column to show whether each of the following statements is true or false.

Answers

1. A component percentage is the percentage relationship between one financial statement item and the total that includes that item. (p. 184)

1. _____

2. The Adequate Disclosure accounting concept is applied when financial statements contain all information necessary to understand a business's financial condition. (p. 180)

2. _____

3. An income statement reports information over a period of time, indicating the financial progress of a business in earning a net income or a net loss. (p. 182)

3. _____

4. The Matching Expenses with Revenue accounting concept is applied when the revenue earned and the expenses incurred to earn that revenue are reported in the same fiscal period. (p. 182)

4. _____

5. Information needed to prepare an income statement comes from the trial balance columns and the income statement columns of a work sheet. (p. 182)

5. _____

6. The income statement for a service business has five sections: heading, revenue, expenses, net income or loss, and capital. (p. 182)

6. _____

7. The work sheet is used to assist in preparing the revenue, expenses, and net income sections of an income statement. (p. 182)

7. _____

8. Only revenue accounts and expense accounts are used in preparing the income statement. (p. 182)

8. _____

9. The net income on an income statement is verified by checking the balance sheet. (p. 183)

9. _____

10. Single lines ruled across an amount column of an income statement indicate that amounts are to be added. (p. 183)

10. _____

11. Component percentages on an income statement are calculated by dividing sales and total expenses by net income. (p. 184)

11. _____

12. All companies should have a total expenses component percentage that is not more than 80.0%. (p. 184)

12. _____

13. When a business has two different sources of revenue, a separate income statement should be prepared for each kind of revenue. (p. 185)

13. _____

14. An amount written in parentheses on a financial statement indicates an estimate. (p. 185)

14. _____

15. A balance sheet reports financial information on a specific date and includes the assets, liabilities, and owner's equity. (p. 187)

15. _____

16. A balance sheet reports information about the elements of the accounting equation. (p. 188)

16. _____

17. The owner's capital amount reported on a balance sheet is calculated as: capital account balance plus drawing account balance, less net income. (p. 189)

17. _____

18. The position of the total asset line is determined after the equities section is prepared. (p. 189)

18. _____

19. Double lines are ruled across the balance sheet columns to show that the column totals have been verified as correct. (p. 189)

19. _____

20. The owner's equity section of a balance sheet may report different kinds of details about owner's equity, depending on the need of the business. (p. 190)

20. _____

Part Two—Analyzing an Income Statement

Directions: The parts of the income statement below are identified with capital letters. Decide the location of each of the following items. Print the letter identifying your choice in the Answers column.

A

B

C

					% OF SALES
D					
E				F	N
G					
H		I			
J				K	O
L				M	P

(pp. 182–184)

Answers

1. Date of the income statement.

1. _____

2. The amount of net income or net loss.

2. _____

3. Business name.

3. _____

4. Expense account balances.

4. _____

5. Expense account titles.

5. _____

6. Heading of expense section.

6. _____

7. Heading of revenue section.

7. _____

8. Net income or net loss component percentage.

8. _____

9. Revenue account title.

9. _____

10. Sales component percentage.

10. _____

11. Statement name.

11. _____

12. Total amount of revenue.

12. _____

13. Total expenses component percentage.

13. _____

14. Words *Net Income* or *Net Loss*.

14. _____

15. Words *Total Expenses*.

15. _____

Part Three—Analyzing Income Statement Procedures

Directions: For each of the following items, select the choice that best completes the statement. Print the letter identifying your choice in the Answers column.

Answers

1. The date on a monthly income statement prepared on July 31 is written as (A) For Month Ended July 31, 20–– (B) July 31, 20–– (C) 20––, July 31 (D) none of the above. (p. 182)

   1. _____

2. Information needed to prepare an income statement's revenue section is obtained from a work sheet's Account Title column and (A) Income Statement Debit column (B) Income Statement Credit column (C) Balance Sheet Debit column (D) Balance Sheet Credit column. (p. 183)

   2. _____

3. Information needed to prepare an income statement's expense section is obtained from a work sheet's Account Title column and (A) Income Statement Debit column (B) Income Statement Credit column (C) Balance Sheet Debit column (D) Balance Sheet Credit column. (p. 183)

   3. _____

4. The amount of net income calculated on an income statement is correct if (A) it is the same as net income shown on the work sheet (B) debits equal credits (C) it is the same as the balance sheet (D) none of the above. (p. 183)

   4. _____

5. The formula for calculating the net income component percentage is (A) net income divided by total sales equals net income component percentage (B) total sales divided by total expenses equals net income component percentage (C) total sales minus total expenses divided by net income equals total net income percentage (D) none of the above. (p. 184)

   5. _____

Study Guide 9

Name	Perfect Score	Your Score
Identifying Accounting Terms	6 Pts.	
Analyzing Accounts Affected by Adjusting and Closing Entries	14 Pts.	
Analyzing Accounts After Closing Entries Are Posted	16 Pts.	
Analyzing Adjusting and Closing Entries	9 Pts.	
Total	45 Pts.	

Part One—Identifying Accounting Terms

Directions: Select the one term in Column I that best fits each definition in Column II. Print the letter identifying your choice in the Answers column.

Column I	Column II	Answers
A. accounting cycle	**1.** Journal entries recorded to update general ledger accounts at the end of a fiscal period. (p. 198)	1. _____
B. adjusting entries	**2.** Accounts used to accumulate information from one fiscal period to the next. (p. 203)	2. _____
C. closing entries	**3.** Accounts used to accumulate information until it is transferred to the owner's capital account. (p. 203)	3. _____
D. permanent accounts	**4.** Journal entries used to prepare temporary accounts for a new fiscal period. (p. 203)	4. _____
E. post-closing trial balance	**5.** A trial balance prepared after the closing entries are posted. (p. 213)	5. _____
F. temporary accounts	**6.** The series of accounting activities included in recording financial information for a fiscal period. (p. 214)	6. _____

Part Two—Analyzing Accounts Affected by Adjusting and Closing Entries

Directions: Use the partial chart of accounts given below. For each adjusting or closing entry described, decide which accounts are debited and credited. Write the account numbers identifying your choice in the proper Answers column.

Account Title	Acct. No.
Supplies	150
Prepaid Insurance	160
Barbara Trevino, Capital	310
Barbara Trevino, Drawing	320
Income Summary	330
Sales	410
Advertising Expense	510
Insurance Expense	520
Supplies Expense	550

Accounts to Be

	Debited	Credited

1–2. Adjusting entry for Supplies. (p. 200)   1. _____   2. _____

3–4. Adjusting entry for Prepaid Insurance. (p. 201)   3. _____   4. _____

5–6. Closing entry for Sales. (p. 205)   5. _____   6. _____

7–8. Closing entry for all expense accounts. (p. 206)   7. _____   8. _____

9–10. Closing entry for Income Summary with a net income. (p. 207)   9. _____   10. _____

11–12. Closing entry for Income Summary with a net loss. (p. 207)   11. _____   12. _____

13–14. Closing entry for owner's drawing account. (p. 208)   13. _____   14. _____

Part Three—Analyzing Accounts After Closing Entries Are Posted (p. 213)

Directions: For each account listed below, decide whether the account will normally appear on a post-closing trial balance. Place a check mark in the proper Answers column to show your answer.

	Appears on a Post-Closing Trial Balance	
	Yes	No
1. Accounts Receivable—J. Land	1. _____	_____
2. Supplies Expense	2. _____	_____
3. Sales	3. _____	_____
4. Miscellaneous Expense	4. _____	_____
5. Prepaid Insurance	5. _____	_____
6. Petty Cash	6. _____	_____
7. Accounts Payable—AA Supplies	7. _____	_____
8. Rent Expense	8. _____	_____
9. Susan Ruff, Drawing	9. _____	_____
10. Supplies	10. _____	_____
11. Cash	11. _____	_____
12. Advertising Expense	12. _____	_____
13. Insurance Expense	13. _____	_____
14. Susan Ruff, Capital	14. _____	_____
15. Income Summary	15. _____	_____
16. Utilities Expense	16. _____	_____

Part Four—Analyzing Adjusting and Closing Entries

Directions: For each of the following items, select the choice that best completes the statement. Print the letter identifying your choice in the Answers column.

Answers

1. Which accounting concept applies when a work sheet is prepared at the end of each fiscal cycle to summarize the general ledger information needed to prepare financial statements? (A) Business Entity (B) Accounting Period Cycle (C) Adequate Disclosure (D) Consistent Reporting. (p. 198)

   1. _____

2. Which accounting concept applies when expenses are reported in the same fiscal period that they are used to produce revenue? (A) Business Entity (B) Going Concern (C) Matching Expenses with Revenue (D) Adequate Disclosure. (p. 200)

   2. _____

3. Information needed for journalizing the adjusting entries is obtained from the (A) general ledger account Balance columns (B) income statement (C) work sheet's Adjustments columns (D) balance sheet. (p. 200)

   3. _____

4. After adjusting entries are posted, the supplies account balance will be equal to (A) the value of supplies used during the fiscal period (B) the value of the supplies on hand at the end of the fiscal period (C) zero (D) none of these. (p. 200)

   4. _____

5. When revenue is greater than total expenses, resulting in a net income, the income summary account has a (A) debit balance (B) credit balance (C) normal debit balance (D) normal credit balance. (p. 204)

   5. _____

6. Information needed for recording the closing entries is obtained from the (A) general ledger accounts' Debit Balance columns (B) work sheet's Income Statement and Balance Sheet columns (C) balance sheet (D) income statement. (p. 204)

   6. _____

7. Income summary is (A) an asset account (B) a liability account (C) a temporary account (D) a permanent account. (p. 205)

   7. _____

8. After the closing entries are posted, the owner's capital account balance should be the same as (A) shown on the balance sheet for the fiscal period (B) shown in the work sheet's Balance Sheet Debit column (C) shown in the work sheet's Balance Sheet Credit column (D) shown in the work sheet's Income Statement Debit column. (p. 208)

   8. _____

9. The accounts listed on a post-closing trial balance are (A) those that have balances after the closing entries are posted (B) all general ledger accounts (C) those that have no balances after adjusting and closing entries (D) those that appear in the work sheet's Trial Balance columns. (p. 213)

   9. _____

Study Guide 10

Name	Perfect Score	Your Score
Identifying Accounting Terms	11 Pts.	
Analyzing Accounting Concepts and Practices	11 Pts.	
Using Columns in an Expanded Journal	48 Pts.	
Total	70 Pts.	

Part One—Identifying Accounting Terms

Directions: Select the one term in Column I that best fits each definition in Column II. Print the letter identifying your choice in the Answers column.

Column I	Column II	Answers
A. cost of merchandise	**1.** A business in which two or more persons combine their assets and skills. (p. 226)	1. _____
B. markup	**2.** Each member of a partnership. (p. 226)	2. _____
C. merchandise	**3.** A business that purchases and sells goods. (p. 228)	3. _____
D. merchandising business	**4.** A merchandising business that sells to those who use or consume the goods. (p. 228)	4. _____
E. partner	**5.** Goods that a merchandising business purchases to sell. (p. 228)	5. _____
F. partnership	**6.** A business that buys and resells merchandise to retail merchandising businesses. (p. 228)	6. _____
G. purchase invoice	**7.** The price a business pays for goods it purchases to sell. (p. 230)	7. _____
H. retail merchandising business	**8.** The amount added to the cost of merchandise to establish the selling price. (p. 230)	8. _____
I. terms of sale	**9.** A business from which merchandise is purchased or supplies or other assets are bought. (p. 230)	9. _____
J. vendor	**10.** An invoice used as a source document for recording a purchase on account transaction. (p. 233)	10. _____
K. wholesale merchandising business	**11.** An agreement between a buyer and a seller about payment for merchandise. (p. 233)	11. _____

Part Two—Analyzing Accounting Concepts and Practices

Directions: Place a *T* for True or an *F* for False in the Answers column to show whether each of the following statements is true or false.

1. Reports and financial records of the business are kept separate from the personal records of the partners. (p. 226)

    1. _____

2. An expanded journal should include a special amount column for every kind of transaction the business might record. (p. 229)

    2. _____

3. The selling price of merchandise must be greater than the cost of merchandise for a business to make a profit. (p. 230)

    3. _____

4. The cost account Purchases is used only to record the value of merchandise purchased. (p. 230)

    4. _____

5. The source document for a cash purchase is a memorandum describing the merchandise purchased. (p. 231)

    5. _____

6. A cash purchase transaction decreases the balance of the cash account. (p. 231)

    6. _____

7. A purchase invoice usually lists only the total cost of the merchandise. (p. 233)

    7. _____

8. A purchase on account transaction increases the balance of the purchases account and increases the balance of the accounts payable account. (p. 234)

    8. _____

9. Buying supplies on account increases the supplies account balance and increases the accounts payable account balance. (p. 236)

    9. _____

10. A cash payment on account transaction increases the accounts payable account balance and decreases the cash account balance. (p. 238)

    10. _____

11. A partner might take merchandise out of the business for personal use. (p. 242)

    11. _____

Part Three—Using Columns in an Expanded Journal

Directions: The columns of the expanded journal below are identified with capital letters. For each transaction below, decide in which column each of the following items should be recorded. Print the letter identifying your choice in the Answers column.

DATE	ACCOUNT TITLE	DOC. NO.	POST. REF.	GENERAL DEBIT	GENERAL CREDIT	ACCOUNTS RECEIVABLE DEBIT	ACCOUNTS RECEIVABLE CREDIT	SALES CREDIT	SALES TAX PAYABLE CREDIT	ACCOUNTS PAYABLE DEBIT	ACCOUNTS PAYABLE CREDIT	PURCHASES DEBIT	CASH DEBIT	CASH CREDIT
A	B	C	D	E	F	G	H	I	J	K	L	M	N	O

Transaction: Purchased merchandise for cash. (p. 231)   **Answers**

1. Date   1. _____
2. Check mark (to show that no account title needs to be written)   2. _____
3. Check number   3. _____
4. Check mark (to show that no individual amounts on this line need to be posted)   4. _____
5. Debit amount   5. _____
6. Credit amount   6. _____

Transaction: Purchased merchandise on account. (p. 234)

7. Date   7. _____
8. Vendor name   8. _____
9. Purchase invoice number   9. _____
10. Debit amount   10. _____
11. Credit amount   11. _____

Transaction: Paid cash for office supplies. (p. 235)

12. Date   12. _____
13. Title of the account debited   13. _____
14. Check number   14. _____
15. Debit amount   15. _____
16. Credit amount   16. _____

Transaction: Bought store supplies on account. (p. 236)

17. Date   17. _____
18. Account title   18. _____
19. Memorandum number   19. _____
20. Debit amount   20. _____
21. Vendor name   21. _____
22. Credit amount   22. _____

JOURNAL

				1 GENERAL	2	3 ACCOUNTS RECEIVABLE	4	5 SALES CREDIT	6 SALES TAX PAYABLE CREDIT	7 ACCOUNTS PAYABLE	8	9 PURCHASES DEBIT	10 CASH	11
DATE	ACCOUNT TITLE	DOC. NO.	POST. REF.	DEBIT	CREDIT	DEBIT	CREDIT			DEBIT	CREDIT		DEBIT	CREDIT
A	B	C	D	E	F	G	H	I	J	K	L	M	N	O

Transaction: Paid cash on account. (p. 238)

23. Date

24. Vendor name

25. Check number

26. Debit amount

27. Credit amount

Transaction: Paid cash for an expense. (p. 239)

28. Date

29. Account title

30. Check number

31. Debit amount

32. Credit amount

Transaction: Paid cash to replenish the petty cash fund: office supplies, advertising, miscellaneous. (p. 240)

33. Date

34. Account titles

35. Check number

36. Debit amounts

37. Credit amount

Transaction: Partner withdrew cash for personal use. (p. 241)

38. Date

39. Account title

40. Check number

41. Debit amount

42. Credit amount

Transaction: Partner withdrew merchandise for personal use. (p. 242)

43. Date

44. Title of the account debited

45. Memorandum number

46. Debit amount

47. Title of the account credited

48. Credit amount

Answers

23. _____

24. _____

25. _____

26. _____

27. _____

28. _____

29. _____

30. _____

31. _____

32. _____

33. _____

34. _____

35. _____

36. _____

37. _____

38. _____

39. _____

40. _____

41. _____

42. _____

43. _____

44. _____

45. _____

46. _____

47. _____

48. _____

Name		Perfect Score	Your Score
	Analyzing Sales and Cash Receipts	27 Pts.	
	Using Columns in an Expanded Journal	18 Pts.	
	Analyzing Sales Tax	5 Pts.	
	Total	50 Pts.	

Part One—Analyzing Sales and Cash Receipts

Directions: Place a *T* for True or an *F* for False in the Answers column to show whether each of the following statements is true or false.

Answers

1. A person or business to whom merchandise or services are sold is a customer. (p. 252)   1. _____
2. Sales tax is a tax on sale of merchandise or services. (p. 252)   2. _____
3. Most states do not require a business to collect sales tax from customers. (p. 252)   3. _____
4. Sales tax rates are usually stated as a percentage of sales. (p. 252)   4. _____
5. The Realization of Revenue accounting concept is applied when a sale is recorded at the time the sale is made. (p. 254)   5. _____
6. A sale of merchandise increases the revenue of a business. (p. 254)   6. _____
7. A credit card sale is a sale in which cash is received for the total amount of the sale at the time of the transaction. (p. 254)   7. _____
8. A cash sale is a sale in which a credit card is used for the total amount of the sale at the time of the transaction. (p. 254)   8. _____
9. At the end of the week, all credit card slips are gathered together, sorted by issuing bank, and mailed individually to each of the banks to collect payment. (p. 254)   9. _____
10. Cash and credit card sales are combined into a single cash sales transaction. (p. 255)   10. _____
11. When cash and credit card sales are recorded at the end of each week, if a month ends in the middle of a week, the whole week is recorded in the following month. (p. 255)   11. _____
12. The source document for a cash sale is a cash register tape. (p. 255)   12. _____
13. For weekly cash and credit card sales, the asset account Cash is debited for the total of sales and sales tax, but the revenue account Sales is credited only for the total of sales. (p. 255)   13. _____
14. The revenue account Sales has a normal credit balance. (p. 255)   14. _____
15. The liability account Sales Tax Payable has a normal debit balance. (p. 255)   15. _____
16. A sale on account is also referred to as a charge sale. (p. 256)   16. _____
17. A sales invoice is also referred to as a sales ticket or a sales slip. (p. 256)   17. _____
18. Charge customer accounts are summarized in a general ledger account titled Accounts Receivable. (p. 257)   18. _____
19. Accounts Receivable is an asset account with a normal debit balance. (p. 257)   19. _____
20. The source document for receiving cash on account is a receipt. (p. 258)   20. _____
21. When cash is received on account, Cash is increased and Accounts Receivable is increased. (p. 258)   21. _____
22. There are two times a journal is proved and ruled: when the journal page is filled and at the end of the month. (p. 260)   22. _____
23. When the totals of a journal page are carried forward, nothing needs to be recorded in the Post. Ref. column on the Carried Forward line. (p. 261)   23. _____
24. When the totals of a journal page are brought forward, nothing needs to be recorded in the Post. Ref. column on the Brought Forward line. (p. 262)   24. _____
25. Equality of debits and credits in a journal and the accuracy of the cash account are proved only at the end of each month. (p. 264)   25. _____
26. Cash is proved when the total of the Cash Debit column equals the total of the Cash Credit column. (p. 264)   26. _____
27. When cash is proved, it must always equal the amount on the next unused check stub. (p. 264)   27. _____

Part Two—Using Columns in an Expanded Journal

Directions: The columns of the expanded journal below are identified with capital letters. For each transaction below, decide in which column each of the following items should be recorded. Print the letter identifying your choice in the Answers column.

					JOURNAL											
				1	2	3	4	5	6	7	8	9	10	11	
DATE	ACCOUNT TITLE	DOC. NO.	POST. REF.	GENERAL		ACCOUNTS RECEIVABLE		SALES CREDIT	SALES TAX PAYABLE CREDIT	ACCOUNTS PAYABLE		PURCHASES DEBIT	CASH		
				DEBIT	CREDIT	DEBIT	CREDIT			DEBIT	CREDIT		DEBIT	CREDIT	
A	B	C	D	E	F	G	H	I	J	K	L	M	N	O	

Transaction: Recorded cash and credit card sales. (p. 255)

1. Date

2. Check mark (to show that no account title needs to be written)

3. Cash register tape number

4. Check mark (to show that no individual amounts on this line need to be posted)

5. Debit amount

6. Credit amount

7. Credit amount

Transaction: Sold merchandise on account. (p. 257)

8. Date

9. Customer name

10. Sales invoice number

11. Debit amount

12. Credit amount

13. Credit amount

Transaction: Received cash on account. (p. 258)

14. Date

15. Customer name

16. Receipt number

17. Debit amount

18. Credit amount

Answers

1. _____
2. _____
3. _____
4. _____
5. _____
6. _____
7. _____

8. _____
9. _____
10. _____
11. _____
12. _____
13. _____

14. _____
15. _____
16. _____
17. _____
18. _____

Part Three—Analyzing Sales Tax

Directions: For each of the following items, select the choice that best completes the statement. Print the letter identifying your choice in the Answers column.

Answers

1. The amount of sales tax collected is recorded in a (A) combined revenue account (B) separate ledger (C) separate liability account (D) separate revenue account. (p. 252)

   1. _____

2. The amount of sales tax on a sale is calculated as price of goods (A) plus the sales tax rate (B) times the sales tax rate (C) minus the sales tax rate (D) divided by the sales tax rate. (p. 252)

   2. _____

3. If a customer buys $300.00 worth of merchandise and the sales tax is 8%, the total bill the customer must pay is (A) $300.00 (B) $308.00 (C) $324.00 (D) $342.00. (p. 252)

   3. _____

4. Sales tax is a liability because (A) it increases the amount of a sale (B) it increases the profit made on a sale (C) the customer must pay it to the retail merchandising business (D) the business must pay the sales tax collected to the government. (p. 252)

   4. _____

5. When merchandise is sold on account and sales tax is also collected, (A) Accounts Receivable is credited for the total sale and sales tax (B) the accounts receivable account balance is increased (C) Sales is debited for the price of the goods (D) the sales tax is not reported. (p. 257)

   5. _____

Study Guide 12

Name		Perfect Score	Your Score
	Identifying Accounting Terms	6 Pts.	
	Analyzing a Journal and Ledgers	15 Pts.	
	Analyzing Posting and Subsidiary Ledgers	10 Pts.	
	Total	31 Pts.	

Part One—Identifying Accounting Terms

Directions: Select the term in Column I that best fits each definition in Column II. Print the letter identifying your choice in the Answers column.

Column I	Column II	Answers
A. accounts payable ledger	1. A ledger that is summarized in a single general ledger account. (p. 274)	1. _____
B. accounts receivable ledger	2. A subsidiary ledger containing only accounts for vendors from whom items are purchased or bought on account. (p. 274)	2. _____
C. controlling account	3. A subsidiary ledger containing only accounts for charge customers. (p. 274)	3. _____
D. schedule of accounts payable	4. An account in a general ledger that summarizes all accounts in a subsidiary ledger. (p. 274)	4. _____
E. schedule of accounts receivable	5. A listing of vendor accounts, account balances, and total amounts due all vendors. (p. 292)	5. _____
F. subsidiary ledger	6. A listing of customer accounts, account balances, and total amount due from all customers. (p. 293)	6. _____

Part Two—Analyzing a Journal and Ledgers

Directions: Place a *T* for True or an *F* for False in the Answers column to show whether each of the following statements is true or false.

Answers

1. When using an accounts receivable ledger, the total amount due from all customers is summarized in a single general ledger account. (p. 274)

1. _____

2. It is usually necessary to have up-to-date balances in the general ledger at all times. (p. 276)

2. _____

3. Frequency of posting to the general ledger is determined by how many accounts are in the chart of accounts. (p. 276)

3. _____

4. Posting does not have to be done at the end of the month. (p. 276)

4. _____

5. Amounts recorded in general amount columns are posted individually to the general ledger account named in the Account Title column. (p. 276)

5. _____

6. Only totals of special amount columns are posted to the general ledger. (p. 277)

6. _____

7. Accounts are arranged in alphabetical order within the subsidiary ledgers. (p. 280)

7. _____

8. A change in the balance of a vendor account also changes the balance of the controlling account Accounts Payable. (p. 280)

8. _____

9. The account form for a vendor has a Credit Balance column because accounts payable are liabilities and liabilities have normal credit balances. (p. 281)

9. _____

10. At the end of the month, the journal's Accounts Payable Debit column total is posted to the controlling account Accounts Payable. (p. 283)

10. _____

11. A change in the balance of a customer account also changes the balance of the controlling account Accounts Receivable. (p. 286)

11. _____

12. Each amount in a journal's Accounts Receivable columns is posted individually to an account in the accounts receivable ledger. (p. 288)

12. _____

13. Each cash receipt on account from a customer is posted as a credit to an account in the accounts receivable ledger. (p. 289)

13. _____

14. An error in posting to a ledger account usually will not affect the trial balance. (p. 292)

14. _____

15. A schedule of accounts payable is prepared before all entries in a journal are posted. (p. 292)

15. _____

Part Three—Analyzing Posting and Subsidiary Ledgers

Directions: For each item below, select the choice that best completes the statement. Print the letter identifying your choice in the Answers column.

Answers

1. The accounts receivable ledger contains an account for (A) a vendor (B) a customer who will pay later (C) a cash customer (D) none of these. (p. 274)

1. _____

2. Each account in a general ledger has (A) two amount columns (B) three amount columns (C) four amount columns (D) none of these. (p. 276)

2. _____

3. Posting the special amount column totals is done (A) weekly (B) daily (C) after each transaction (D) none of these. (p. 277)

3. _____

4. A check mark is placed in parentheses below the General Debit and General Credit column totals in the journal to indicate that the two column totals are (A) posted individually (B) posted only as part of the column total (C) not posted (D) none of these. (p. 278)

4. _____

5. Totals of the Accounts Payable special amount columns are posted to the general ledger (A) daily (B) weekly (C) at the end of the month (D) none of these. (p. 282)

5. _____

6. When a credit is posted to the accounts payable ledger, the (A) previous balance is added to the new amount posted in the Credit column (B) source document number and page number of the journal are written in the Post. Ref. column of the account (C) credit amount is written in the Debit column of the account (D) word *Balance* is written in the Item column. (p. 282)

6. _____

7. When a debit is posted to the accounts payable ledger, the (A) debit amount is written in the Debit column of the account (B) cash account increases (C) controlling account is increased by the entry (D) all of the above. (p. 283)

7. _____

8. The total of all customer account balances in the accounts receivable ledger equals (A) the balance in the accounts receivable controlling account (B) the balance in the accounts payable controlling account (C) the cash account (D) none of these. (p. 286)

8. _____

9. The separate amounts in the Accounts Receivable Debit column of a journal are (A) posted individually to the general ledger (B) posted to the general ledger only as a part of the column total (C) not posted to the general ledger (D) none of these. (p. 288)

9. _____

10. When opening a new page in an accounts receivable ledger, (A) *Balance* is written in the Item column (B) the Item column is left blank (C) a number is written in the Post. Ref. column (D) none of these. (p. 289)

10. _____

Study Guide 13

Name	Perfect Score	Your Score
Identifying Accounting Terms	12 Pts.	
Analyzing Payroll Procedures	5 Pts.	
Identifying Accounting Practices	20 Pts.	
Total	37 Pts.	

Part One—Identifying Accounting Terms

Directions: Select the one term in Column I that best fits each definition in Column II. Print the letter identifying your choice in the Answers column.

Column I	Column II	Answers
A. employee earnings record	1. The money paid for employee services. (p. 302)	1. _____
B. Medicare tax	2. The period covered by a salary payment. (p. 302)	2. _____
C. net pay	3. The total amount earned by all employees for a pay period. (p. 302)	3. _____
D. pay period	4. The total pay due for a pay period before deductions. (p. 306)	4. _____
E. payroll	5. Taxes based on the payroll of a business. (p. 308)	5. _____
F. payroll register	6. A deduction from total earnings for each person legally supported by a taxpayer, including the employee. (p. 309)	6. _____
G. payroll taxes	7. A federal tax paid for old-age, survivors, and disability insurance. (p. 312)	7. _____
H. salary	8. A federal tax paid for hospital insurance. (p. 312)	8. _____
I. social security tax	9. The maximum amount of earnings on which a tax is calculated. (p. 312)	9. _____
J. tax base	10. A business form used to record payroll information. (p. 314)	10. _____
K. total earnings	11. The total earnings paid to an employee after payroll taxes and other deductions. (p. 315)	11. _____
L. withholding allowance	12. A business form used to record details affecting payments made to an employee. (p. 316)	12. _____

Part Two—Analyzing Payroll Procedures

Directions: For each of the following items, select the choice that best completes the statement. Print the letter of your choice in the Answers column.

1. How many hours were worked by an employee who arrived at 8:10 a.m. and departed at 12:10 p.m.? (A) 4 hours (B) 5 hours (C) 4 hours and ten minutes (D) none of these. (p. 305)

   1._____

2. How many hours were worked by an employee who arrived at 7:05 a.m. and departed at 6:05 p.m. with one hour off for lunch? (A) 11 hours (B) 10 hours (C) 12 hours (D) none of these. (p. 305)

   2._____

3. Employee regular earnings are calculated as (A) regular hours times regular rate (B) total hours divided by regular rate (C) total hours plus overtime rate (D) overtime hours minus overtime rate. (p. 306)

   3._____

4. Information needed to determine the employee social security tax withholding for a pay period includes (A) total earnings and social security tax rate (B) total earnings and accumulated earnings (C) total earnings, number of withholding allowances, and social security tax rate (D) total earnings, accumulated earnings, and social security tax rate and tax base. (p. 312)

   4._____

5. A separate payroll checking account is used primarily to (A) simplify the payroll accounting system (B) help reduce the cost of preparing a payroll (C) eliminate employer earnings records (D) provide additional protection and control of individual payroll checks. (p. 319)

   5._____

Part Three—Identifying Accounting Practices

Directions: Place a *T* for True or an *F* for False in the Answers column to
show whether each of the following statements is true or false.

Answers

1. A business may decide to pay employee salaries every week, every two weeks, twice a month, or once a month. (p. 302)

   1. _____

2. Businesses use payroll records to inform employees of their annual earnings and to prepare payroll reports for the government. (p. 302)

   2. _____

3. Payroll time cards can be used as the basic source of information to prepare a payroll. (p. 304)

   3. _____

4. The first task in preparing a payroll is to determine the number of days worked by each employee. (p. 305)

   4. _____

5. Total earnings are sometimes referred to as net pay or net earnings. (p. 306)

   5. _____

6. Employee total earnings are calculated as regular hours × regular rate, plus overtime hours × overtime rate. (p. 306)

   6. _____

7. Payroll taxes are based on employee total earnings. (p. 308)

   7. _____

8. A business is required by law to withhold certain payroll taxes from employee salaries. (p. 308)

   8. _____

9. Employers in many states are required to withhold state, city, or county income tax from employee earnings. (p. 308)

   9. _____

10. Payroll taxes withheld represent a liability for an employer until payment is made. (p. 308)

   10. _____

11. Federal law requires that each employer have on file a properly completed Form W-2, Employee's Withholding Allowance Certificate, for each employee. (p. 309)

   11. _____

12. The amount of income tax withheld from each employee's total earnings is determined from the number of withholding allowances and by the employee's marital status. (p. 309)

   12. _____

13. A single person will have less income tax withheld than a married employee. (p. 309)

   13. _____

14. An employee can be exempt from having federal income tax withheld under certain conditions. (p. 309)

   14. _____

15. Social security tax is paid by the employer only. (p. 312)

   15. _____

16. An act of Congress can change the social security tax base and tax rate at any time. (p. 312)

   16. _____

17. When an employee's earnings exceed the tax base, no more social security tax is deducted. (p. 312)

   17. _____

18. All deductions from employee wages are recorded in a payroll register. (p. 315)

   18. _____

19. The columns of the employee earnings record consist of the amount columns in a payroll register and an accumulated earnings column. (p. 317)

   19. _____

20. The information used to prepare payroll checks is taken from a payroll register. (p. 320)

   20. _____

Study Guide 14

Name	Perfect Score	Your Score
Analyzing Payroll Records	15 Pts.	
Analyzing Transactions Affecting Payroll	5 Pts.	
Analyzing Form W-2	10 Pts.	
Total	30 Pts.	

Part One—Analyzing Payroll Records

Directions: For each of the following items, select the choice that best completes the statement. Print the letter identifying your choice in the Answers column.

Answers

1. All the payroll information needed to prepare a payroll and tax reports is found on (A) Form W-4 and the employee earnings record (B) Form W-4 and the payroll register (C) the payroll register and the employee earnings record (D) Form W-4. (p. 330)

1. _____

2. The payroll journal entry is based on the totals of (A) Earnings Total column, each deduction column, and Net Pay column (B) Earnings Total, Earnings Regular, Earnings Overtime, and Deductions Total columns (C) Earnings Regular, Earnings Overtime, and Deductions Total columns (D) Earnings Total, Earnings Regular, and Earnings Overtime Total columns. (p. 332)

2. _____

3. The total of the Net Pay column of the payroll register is credited to (A) a revenue account (B) an expense account (C) an asset account (D) a liability account. (p. 333)

3. _____

4. When a semimonthly payroll is paid, the credit to Cash is equal to the (A) total earnings of all employees (B) total deductions for income tax and social security tax (C) total deductions (D) net pay of all employees. (p. 333)

4. _____

5. The Total Earnings column total is journalized as a debit to (A) Cash (B) Salary Expense (C) Employee Income Tax Payable (D) Social Security Tax Payable. (p. 333)

5. _____

6. The total of the Federal Income Tax column of a payroll register is credited to (A) a revenue account (B) an expense account (C) a liability account (D) an asset account. (p. 333)

6. _____

7. A business's payroll taxes for a pay period are debited to (A) an asset account (B) a liability account (C) a revenue account (D) an expense account. (p. 336)

7. _____

8. Payroll taxes that are paid by both the employer and the employee are (A) federal unemployment tax and social security tax (B) federal unemployment tax and Medicare tax (C) social security tax and Medicare tax (D) federal income tax, social security tax, and Medicare tax. (p. 336)

8. _____

9. A federal tax used for state and federal administrative expenses of the unemployment program is (A) social security tax (B) Medicare tax (C) federal unemployment tax (D) state unemployment tax. (p. 338)

9. _____

10. A state tax used to pay benefits to unemployed workers is (A) social security tax (B) Medicare tax (C) unemployment tax (D) state unemployment tax. (p. 338))

10. _____

11. To record the employer payroll taxes expense, the following accounts are credited: (A) Payroll Taxes Expense and Employee Income Tax Payable (B) Employee Income Tax Payable, Social Security Tax Payable, Medicare Tax Payable, Unemployment Tax Payable—Federal, and Unemployment Tax Payable—State (C) Social Security Tax Payable, Medicare Tax Payable, Unemployment Tax Payable—Federal, and Unemployment Tax Payable—State (D) none of these. (p. 339)

11. _____

12. Each employer who withholds income tax, social security tax, and Medicare tax from employee earnings must furnish each employee an (A) IRS Form W-4 (B) IRS Form W-2 (C) IRS Form W-3 (D) IRS Form 941. (p. 341)

12. _____

13. Each employer is required by law to report payroll taxes on an (A) IRS Form W-4 (B) IRS Form 941 (C) IRS Form W-2 (D) IRS Form W-3. (p. 343)

13. _____

14. To record the total federal tax payment for employee income tax, social security tax, and Medicare tax, the account credited is (A) Cash (B) Employee Income Tax Payable (C) Social Security Tax Payable (D) Medicare Tax Payable. (p. 348)

14. _____

15. To record the payment of federal unemployment tax, the account debited is (A) a revenue account (B) an expense account (C) a liability account (D) an asset account. (p. 350)

15. _____

Part Two—Analyzing Transactions Affecting Payroll

Directions: Analyze each of the following transactions into debit and credit parts. Print the letters identifying your choices in the proper Answers column.

Account Title	Transaction	Debit	Credit
A. Cash	**1.** Paid cash for semimonthly payroll. (p. 334)	_____	_____
B. Employee Income Tax Payable	**2.** Recorded employer payroll taxes expense. (p. 339)	_____	_____
C. Medicare Tax Payable	**3.** Paid cash for liability for employee income tax, social security tax, and Medicare tax. (p. 348)	_____	_____
D. Payroll Taxes Expense	**4.** Paid cash for federal unemployment tax liability. (p. 350)	_____	_____
E. Salary Expense	**5.** Paid cash for state unemployment tax liability. (p. 350)	_____	_____
F. Social Security Tax Payable			
G. Unemployment Tax Payable—Federal			
H. Unemployment Tax Payable—State			

Part Three—Analyzing Form W-2

Directions: Analyze the following statements about a Form W-2, Wage and Tax Statement. Use the Form W-2 below to answer the specific questions about Rick Selby. Place a *T* for True or an *F* for False in the Answers column to show whether each of the following statements is true or false. (p. 341)

a Control number 22222	Void ☐	For Official Use Only ▶ OMB No. 1545-0008	
b Employer's identification number 31-0429632		1 Wages, tips, other compensation 24,843.00	2 Federal income tax withheld 1,152.00
c Employer's name, address, and ZIP code		3 Social security wages 24,843.00	4 Social security tax withheld 1,614.80
Omni Import 1374 Parklane Ashton, RI 02805		5 Medicare wages and tips 24,843.00	6 Medicare tax withheld 372.65
		7 Social security tips	8 Allocated tips
d Employee's social security number 450-70-6432		9 Advanced EIC payment	10 Dependent care benefits
e Employee's name (first, middle initial, last) Rick E. Selby		11 Nonqualified plans	12 Benefits included in box 1
1625 Northland Drive Ashton, RI 02805		13 See Instrs. for box 13	14 Other

15	Statutory employee ☐	Deceased ☐	Pension plan ☐	Legal rep. ☐	Hshld. emp. ☐	Subtotal ☐	Deferred compensation ☐

16 State	Employer's state I.D. No.	17 State wages, tips, etc.	18 State income tax	19 Locality name	20 Local wages, tips, etc.	21 Local income tax

39-1754529 Department of the Treasury—Internal Revenue Service
For Paperwork Reduction Act Notice, see separate instructions.

Form **W-2** Wage and Tax Statement **20—**
Copy A For Social Security Administration

Answers

1. Rick Selby's total salary is more than his total social security salary. 1. _____

2. This form W-2 shows Rick Selby's net pay for the entire year. 2. _____

3. The amount withheld for Mr. Selby's social security and Medicare tax was more than the amount withheld for his federal income tax. 3. _____

4. If an employee works for several employers during the year, that employee must receive a Form W-2 from each employer. 4. _____

5. When Rick Selby files his federal income tax return, he must attach Copy A of his Form W-2 to his return. 5. _____

6. An employer is required to provide employees with a Form W-2 no later than January 1 of the year following the one for which the report has been completed. 6. _____

7. All deductions from Mr. Selby's salary are shown on his Form W-2. 7. _____

8. State income tax was withheld from Mr. Selby's salary. 8. _____

9. This Form W-2 would indicate whether Mr. Selby had more than one employer during the year. 9. _____

10. An employee's social security number must be shown on all copies of his or her Form W-2. 10. _____

Study Guide 15

Name	Perfect Score	Your Score
Analyzing Adjustments on a Work Sheet	10 Pts.	
Analyzing Work Sheet Extensions	34 Pts.	
Total	44 Pts.	

Part One—Analyzing Adjustments on a Work Sheet

Directions: For each of the following items, select the choice that best completes the statement. Print the letter identifying your choice in the Answers column.

Answers

1. The Merchandise Inventory amount in a work sheet's Trial Balance Debit column represents the merchandise inventory (A) at the end of a fiscal period (B) at the beginning of a fiscal period (C) purchased during a fiscal period (D) available during a fiscal period. (p. 368)

1. _____

2. The amount of goods on hand is called (A) purchases (B) sales (C) inventory (D) merchandise inventory. (p. 368)

2. _____

3. The amount of goods on hand for sale to customers is called (A) inventory (B) purchases (C) sales (D) merchandise inventory. (p. 368)

3. _____

4. The Income Summary amount in a work sheet's Adjustments Debit column represents the (A) decrease in Merchandise Inventory (B) increase in Merchandise Inventory (C) beginning Merchandise Inventory (D) ending Merchandise Inventory. (p. 369)

4. _____

5. The two accounts used to adjust the Merchandise Inventory account are (A) Merchandise Inventory and Supplies (B) Merchandise Inventory and Purchases (C) Merchandise Inventory and Income Summary (D) Merchandise Inventory and Sales. (p. 369)

5. _____

6. The Supplies—Office amount in a work sheet's Trial Balance Debit column represents the value of supplies (A) at the beginning of a fiscal period (B) used during a fiscal period (C) at the beginning of a fiscal period plus office supplies bought during the fiscal period (D) bought during a fiscal period. (p. 373)

6. _____

7. Recording expenses in the accounting period in which the expenses contribute to earning revenue is an application of the accounting concept (A) Matching Expenses with Revenue (B) Consistent Reporting (C) Historical Cost (D) Adequate Disclosure. (p. 373)

7. _____

8. The two accounts used to adjust the Office Supplies account are (A) Supplies and Purchases (B) Supplies—Office and Income Summary (C) Supplies—Office and Supplies Expense—Office (D) Supplies Expense—Office and Income Summary. (p. 373)

8. _____

9. The portion of the insurance premiums that has expired during a fiscal period is classified as (A) a liability (B) an asset (C) an expense (D) capital. (p. 375)

9. _____

10. The two accounts used to adjust the Prepaid Insurance account are (A) Insurance Expense and Income Summary (B) Prepaid Insurance and Insurance Expense (C) Prepaid Insurance and Income Summary (D) Prepaid Insurance Expense and Income Summary. (p. 375)

10. _____

Part Two—Analyzing Work Sheet Extensions (p. 378)

Directions: For each account listed below, place a check mark in the column to which amounts are extended on a work sheet.

Account Title	Income Statement Debit	Income Statement Credit	Balance Sheet Debit	Balance Sheet Credit
1. Accounts Payable				
2. Accounts Receivable				
3. Advertising Expense				
4. Cash				
5. Credit Card Fee Expense				
6. Employee Income Tax Payable				
7. Health Insurance Premiums Payable				
8. Income Summary (ending inventory smaller than beginning inventory)				
9. Insurance Expense				
10. Karl Koehn, Capital				
11. Karl Koehn, Drawing				
12. Medicare Tax Payable				
13. Merchandise Inventory				
14. Michelle Wu, Capital				
15. Michelle Wu, Drawing				
16. Miscellaneous Expense				
17. Payroll Taxes Expense				
18. Petty Cash				
19. Prepaid Insurance				
20. Purchases				
21. Rent Expense				
22. Salary Expense				
23. Sales				
24. Sales Tax Payable				
25. Social Security Tax Payable				
26. Supplies Expense—Office				
27. Supplies Expense—Store				
28. Supplies—Office				
29. Supplies—Store				
30. Unemployment Tax Payable—Federal				
31. Unemployment Tax Payable—State				
32. United Way Donations Payable				
33. U.S. Savings Bonds Payable				
34. Utilities Expense				

Study Guide 16

Name	Perfect Score	Your Score
Identifying Accounting Terms	5 Pts.	
Analyzing Acceptable Component Percentages	8 Pts.	
Analyzing Financial Statements for a Merchandising Business	20 Pts.	
Total	33 Pts.	

Part One—Identifying Accounting Terms

Directions: Select the one term in Column I that best fits each definition in Column II. Print the letter identifying your choice in the Answers column.

Column I	**Column II**	**Answers**
A. cost of merchandise sold	1. The total original price of all merchandise sold during a fiscal period. (p. 382)	1. _____
B. distribution of net income statement	2. The revenue remaining after cost of merchandise sold has been deducted. (p. 384)	2. _____
C. gross profit on sales	3. A partnership financial statement showing net income or loss distribution to partners. (p. 402)	3. _____
D. owners' equity statement	4. A financial statement that summarizes the changes in owners' equity during a fiscal period. (p. 404)	4. _____
E. supporting schedule	5. A report prepared to give details about an item on a principal financial statement. (p. 411)	5. _____

Part Two—Analyzing Acceptable Component Percentages

Directions: For each of the income statement component percentages given, write a *U* in the Answers column if it is Unacceptable and write an *A* in the Answers column if it is Acceptable. (pp. 397–398)

Acceptable Component Percentages	
Sales	100%
Cost of merchandise sold	Not more than 48.6%
Gross profit on sales	Not less than 51.4%
Total expenses	Not more than 34.9%
Net income	Not less than 16.5%

Answers

1. The component percentage for total expenses is 42.8% this year.

1. _____

2. The component percentage for cost of merchandise sold is 51.0% this year.

2. _____

3. The component percentage for gross profit on sales is 52.8% this year.

3. _____

4. The component percentage for total expenses is 34.3% this year.

4. _____

5. The component percentage for gross profit on sales is 51.4% this year.

5. _____

6. The component percentage for net income is 17.0% this year.

6. _____

7. The component percentage for cost of merchandise sold is 48.7% this year.

7. _____

8. The component percentage for net income is 10.4% this year.

8. _____

Part Three—Analyzing Financial Statements for a Merchandising Business

Directions: Place a *T* for True or an *F* for False in the Answers column to show whether each of the following statements is true or false.

Answers

1. Financial statements provide the primary source of information needed by owners and managers to make decisions on the future activity of a business. (p. 390)

1. _____

2. Reporting financial information the same way from one fiscal period to the next is an application of the accounting concept Adequate Disclosure. (p. 390)

2. _____

3. An income statement is used to report a business's financial progress. (p. 392)

3. _____

4. An income statement for a merchandising business has three main sections: revenue section, cost of merchandise sold section, and expenses section. (p. 392)

4. _____

5. The data for the revenue section of the income statement are obtained from the work sheet's Income Statement Credit column. (p. 393)

5. _____

6. Revenue less cost of merchandise sold equals net income. (p. 394)

6. _____

7. Total expenses on an income statement are deducted from the gross profit on sales to find net income. (p. 395)

7. _____

8. For a merchandising business, every sales dollar reported on the income statement includes only three components: gross profit on sales, total expenses, and net income. (p. 397)

8. _____

9. When a business's expenses are less than the gross profit on sales, the difference is known as a net loss. (p. 399)

9. _____

10. Increasing sales revenue while keeping cost of merchandise sold the same will increase gross profit on sales. (p. 400)

10. _____

11. Most businesses correct an unacceptable component percentage for gross profit by simply increasing the markup on merchandise purchased for sale because an increased selling price will always increase profit. (p. 400)

11. _____

12. Net income is shown on the last line of a distribution of net income statement. (p. 402)

12. _____

13. A separate financial statement may be prepared to show the distribution of net income or loss to partners. (p. 402)

13. _____

14. A partnership's net income or net loss must be divided equally by the partners. (p. 402)

14. _____

15. A distribution of net income statement summarizes how owner's equity has changed during a fiscal period. (p. 404)

15. _____

16. Owner's equity can be changed only when a partner withdraws cash or other assets from the business or makes an additional investment in the business. (p. 404)

16. _____

17. The owner's equity in a business is affected when a business earns an income or incurs a loss. (p. 404)

17. _____

18. Data needed to prepare the liabilities section of a balance sheet are obtained from a work sheet's Balance Sheet Debit column. (pp. 408–409)

18. _____

19. Ruled double lines across both amount columns below Total Assets and below Total Liabilities and Owners' Equity show that the amounts have been verified as correct. (p. 410)

19. _____

20. When more detailed information about an item on a financial statement is needed, a supporting schedule may be prepared. (p. 411)

20. _____

Name		Perfect Score	Your Score
Analyzing Accounts Affected by Adjusting and Closing Entries		22 Pts.	
Examining Adjusting and Closing Entries		18 Pts.	
	Total	40 Pts.	

Part One—Analyzing Accounts Affected by Adjusting and Closing Entries

Directions: For each adjusting or closing entry described, decide which accounts are debited and credited. Print the letter identifying your choice in the proper Answers column.

		Accounts to Be	
Account Title	**Transaction**	**Debited**	**Credited**
A. Advertising Expense	**1–2.** Adjusting entry for a decrease in merchandise inventory. (p. 423)	_____	_____
B. Heather Haws, Capital	**3–4.** Adjusting entry for office supplies. (p. 424)	_____	_____
C. Heather Haws, Drawing	**5–6.** Adjusting entry for prepaid insurance. (p. 424)	_____	_____
D. Income Summary	**7–8.** Closing entry for the sales account. (p. 427)	_____	_____
E. Insurance Expense	**9–10.** Closing entry for the purchases account. (p. 429)	_____	_____
F. Merchandise Inventory	**11–12.** Closing entry for the advertising expense account. (p. 429)	_____	_____
G. Prepaid Insurance	**13–14.** Closing entry for the office supplies expense account. (p. 429)	_____	_____
H. Purchases	**15–16.** Closing entry for the insurance expense account. (p. 429)	_____	_____
I. Sales	**17–18.** Closing entry for the income summary account with a net income. (p. 431)	_____	_____
J. Supplies—Office	**19–20.** Closing entry for the income summary account with a net loss. (p. 431)	_____	_____
K. Supplies Expense—Office	**21–22.** Closing entry for the partners' drawing accounts. (p. 432)	_____	_____
L. Hank Haws, Capital			
M. Hank Haws, Drawing			

Part Two—Examining Adjusting and Closing Entries

Directions: Place a *T* for True or an *F* for False in the Answers column to show whether each of the following statements is true or false.

Answers

1. General ledger account balances are changed only by posting journal entries. (p. 420)
   1. _____

2. Adjusting entries bring subsidiary ledger accounts up to date. (p. 420)
   2. _____

3. Adjusting entries are recorded in a journal on the next line following the last daily transaction. (p. 422)
   3. _____

4. Indicating a source document is not necessary when journalizing adjusting entries. (p. 422)
   4. _____

5. A prepaid insurance adjustment includes a debit to Insurance Expense and a credit to Prepaid Insurance. (p. 424)
   5. _____

6. Temporary accounts are closed at the end of a fiscal period to prepare the general ledger for the next fiscal period. (p. 426)
   6. _____

7. The Trial Balance columns of a work sheet and a distribution of net income statement contain the information needed to journalize closing entries. (p. 426)
   7. _____

8. A temporary account is closed by transferring its balance out of the account. (p. 426)
   8. _____

9. Revenue accounts are transferred to the credit side of the income summary account. (p. 427)
   9. _____

10. Closing the revenue account at the end of a fiscal period is an application of the accounting concept Matching Expenses with Revenue. (p. 427)
    10. _____

11. Expense accounts are closed by debiting the expense accounts and crediting Income Summary. (p. 428)
    11. _____

12. The income summary account is closed into the capital accounts. (p. 431)
    12. _____

13. A closing entry is made to close the drawing accounts into Income Summary. (p. 432)
    13. _____

14. After all closing entries are posted, the balances of the partners' capital accounts equal the amounts reported in the owners' section of the balance sheet. (p. 432)
    14. _____

15. After all closing entries are posted, the income statement accounts are the only general ledger accounts that have balances. (p. 435)
    15. _____

16. After all closing entries are posted, the temporary accounts have zero balances. (p. 435)
    16. _____

17. The purpose of the post-closing trial balance is to prove the general ledger equality of debits and credits. (p. 437)
    17. _____

18. When the general ledger is ready for the next fiscal period, this is an application of the Business Entity accounting concept. (p. 437)
    18. _____

Study Guide 18

Name		Perfect Score	Your Score
	Identifying Accounting Terms	17 Pts.	
	Analyzing Purchases and Cash Payments	7 Pts.	
	Analyzing Transactions Recorded in Special Journals	24 Pts.	
	Analyzing Special Journals	12 Pts.	
	Total	60 Pts.	

Part One—Identifying Accounting Terms

Directions: Select the term in Column I that best fits each definition in Column II. Print the letter identifying your choice in the Answers column.

Column I	Column II	Answers
A. capital stock	1. An organization with the legal rights of a person and which may be owned by many persons. (p. 454)	1. _____
B. cash discount	2. Each unit of ownership in a corporation. (p. 454)	2. _____
C. cash over	3. Total shares of ownership in a corporation. (p. 454)	3. _____
D. cash payments journal	4. A journal used to record only one kind of transaction. (p. 455)	4. _____
E. cash short	5. A special journal used to record only purchases of merchandise on account transactions. (p. 455)	5. _____
F. contra account	6. A special journal used to record only cash payment transactions. (p. 460)	6. _____
G. corporation	7. A business's printed or catalog price. (p. 461)	7. _____
H. debit memorandum	8. A reduction in the list price granted to customers. (p. 461)	8. _____
I. general journal	9. A deduction that a vendor allows on the invoice amount to encourage prompt payment. (p. 462)	9. _____
J. list price	10. A cash discount on purchases taken by a customer. (p. 462)	10. _____
K. purchases allowance	11. An account that reduces a related account on a financial statement. (p. 462)	11. _____
L. purchases discount	12. A petty cash on hand amount that is less than a recorded amount. (p. 465)	12. _____
M. purchases journal	13. A petty cash on hand amount that is more than a recorded amount. (p. 465)	13. _____
N. purchases return	14. A journal with two amount columns in which all kinds of entries can be recorded. (p. 470)	14. _____
O. share of stock	15. Credit allowed for the purchase price of returned merchandise, resulting in a decrease in the customer's accounts payable. (p. 471)	15. _____
P. special journal	16. Credit allowed for part of the purchase price of merchandise that is not returned, resulting in a decrease in the customer's accounts payable. (p. 471)	16. _____
Q. trade discount	17. A form prepared by the customer showing the price deduction taken by the customer for returns and allowances. (p. 471)	17. _____

Part Two—Analyzing Purchases and Cash Payments

Directions: Place a *T* for True or an *F* for False in the Answers column to show whether each of the following statements is true or false.

Answers

1. When purchases are recorded at their cost, including any related shipping costs and taxes, the Historical Cost accounting concept is being applied. (p. 456)

    1. _____

2. Trade discounts are recorded in the purchases discount account. (p. 461)

    2. _____

3. The terms of sale l/10, n/30 mean that the customer may deduct 1% of the invoice amount if payment is made within 30 days of the invoice date. (p. 462)

    3. _____

4. The terms of sale 2/15, n/30 mean that 2% of the invoice amount may be deducted if paid within 15 days of the invoice date or the total invoice amount must be paid within 30 days. (p. 462)

    4. _____

5. Purchases discounts are subtracted from the purchases journal total. (p. 462)

    5. _____

6. The source document for a purchases return is a check. (p. 471)

    6. _____

7. A contra purchases account has a normal credit balance. (p. 472)

    7. _____

Part Three—Analyzing Transactions Recorded in Special Journals

Directions: In Answers Column l, print the abbreviation for the journal in which each transaction is to be recorded. In Answers Columns 2 and 3, print the letters identifying the accounts to be debited and credited for each transaction.

P—Purchases journal   G—General journal   CP—Cash payments journal

Account Titles	Transactions	Journal	Answers Debit	Credit
A. Accounts Payable	1–2–3. Purchased merchandise on account from Warren Clubs. (p. 456)	1. _____	2. _____	3. _____
B. Cash	4–5–6. Paid cash for rent. (p. 460)	4. _____	5. _____	6. _____
C. Cash Short and Over	7–8–9. Purchased merchandise for cash. (p. 461)	7. _____	8. _____	9. _____
D. Miscellaneous Expense	10–11–12. Paid cash on account to Warren Clubs, less purchases discount. (p. 462)	10. _____	11. _____	12. _____
E. Petty Cash	13–14–15. Paid cash on account to Trice Company. (p. 463)	13. _____	14. _____	15. _____
F. Purchases	16–17–18. Paid cash to replenish the petty cash fund: supplies, miscellaneous, cash over. (p. 466)	16. _____	17. _____	18. _____
G. Purchases Discount	19–20–21. Returned merchandise to Trice Company. (p. 472)	19. _____	20. _____	21. _____
H. Purchases Returns and Allowances	22–23–24. Bought supplies on account from Wright Supplies. (p. 473)	22. _____	23. _____	24. _____
I. Rent Expense				
J. Supplies				
K. Trice Company				
L. Warren Clubs				
M. Wright Supplies				

Part Four—Analyzing Special Journals

Directions: Place a *T* for True or an *F* for False in the Answers column to show whether each of the following statements is true or false.

Answers

1. As in proprietorships and partnerships, information in a corporation's accounting system is kept separate from the personal records of the owners, and this accounting concept application is called a business entity. (p. 454)

   1. _____

2. A corporation can incur liabilities but cannot own property. (p. 454)

   2. _____

3. All transactions recorded in a purchases journal increase the balance of a vendor account. (p. 456)

   3. _____

4. Each amount in the amount column of a purchases journal is posted individually as a credit to a vendor account in the accounts payable ledger. (p. 457)

   4. _____

5. The monthly total of a purchases journal is posted as a credit to Purchases. (p. 458)

   5. _____

6. All transactions recorded in a purchases journal increase the balance of the purchases account. (p. 458)

   6. _____

7. When a cash payments journal is used, all payments of cash are recorded in it. (p. 460)

   7. _____

8. Purchases on account are recorded in a purchases journal at list price. (p. 461)

   8. _____

9. Each amount in the Accounts Payable Debit column of a cash payments journal is posted individually to the account named in the Account Title column. (p. 467)

   9. _____

10. The monthly total of the General Debit column of a cash payments journal is posted to the general ledger. (p. 467)

   10. _____

11. The amount recorded in the Debit column of a general journal for a purchases return must be posted to two different accounts. (p. 472)

   11. _____

12. Buying supplies on account is recorded in the general journal. (p. 473)

   12. _____

Study Guide 19

Name		Perfect Score	Your Score
	Identifying Accounting Terms	16 Pts.	
	Analyzing Transactions Recorded in Special Journals	24 Pts.	
	Analyzing Sales and Cash Receipts	10 Pts.	
	Total	50 Pts.	

Part One—Identifying Accounting Terms

Directions: Select the term in Column I that best fits each definition in Column II. Print the letter identifying your choice in the Answers column.

Column I	Column II	Answers
A. bill of lading	1. A special journal used to record only sales of merchandise on account transactions. (p. 488)	1. _____
B. cash receipts journal	2. A special journal used to record only cash receipt transactions. (p. 493)	2. _____
C. commercial invoice	3. A cash discount on sales. (p. 494)	3. _____
D. contract of sale	4. Credit allowed a customer for the sales price of returned merchandise, resulting in a decrease in the vendor's accounts receivable. (p. 499)	4. _____
E. credit memorandum	5. Credit allowed a customer for part of the sales price of merchandise that is not returned, resulting in a decrease in the vendor's accounts receivable. (p. 499)	5. _____
F. draft	6. A form prepared by the vendor showing the amount deducted for returns and allowances. (p. 499)	6. _____
G. exports	7. Goods or services shipped out of a seller's home country to a foreign country. (p. 504)	7. _____
H. imports	8. Goods or services bought from a foreign country and brought into a buyer's home country. (p. 504)	8. _____
I. letter of credit	9. A document that details all the terms agreed to by seller and buyer for a sales transaction. (p. 505)	9. _____
J. sales allowance	10. A letter issued by a bank guaranteeing that a named individual or business will be paid a specified amount, provided stated conditions are met. (p. 505)	10. _____
K. sales discount	11. A receipt signed by the authorized agent of a transportation company for merchandise received that also serves as a contract for the delivery of the merchandise. (p. 505)	11. _____
L. sales journal	12. A statement prepared by the seller of merchandise addressed to the buyer, showing a detailed listing and description of merchandise sold, including prices and terms. (p. 505)	12. _____
M. sales return	13. A written, signed, and dated order from one party ordering another party, usually a bank, to pay money to a third party. (p. 505)	13. _____
N. sight draft	14. A draft payable on sight, when the holder presents it for payment. (p. 505)	14. _____
O. time draft	15. A draft that is payable at a fixed or determinable future time after it is accepted. (p. 507)	15. _____
P. trade acceptance	16. A form signed by a buyer at the time of a sale of merchandise, in which the buyer promises to pay the seller a specified sum of money, usually at a stated time in the future. (p. 508)	16. _____

Part Two—Analyzing Transactions Recorded in Special Journals

Directions: In Answers Column 1, print the abbreviation for the journal in which each transaction is to be recorded. In Answers Columns 2 and 3, print the letters identifying the accounts to be debited and credited for each transaction.

S—Sales journal   G—General journal   CR—Cash receipts journal

Account Title	Transaction	Journal	Answers Debit	Credit
A. Accounts Receivable	1–2–3. Sold merchandise on account to Laura Lawton, plus sales tax. (p. 489)	1. _____	2. _____	3. _____
B. Cash	4–5–6. Recorded cash and credit card sales, plus sales tax. (p. 493)	4. _____	5. _____	6. _____
C. Laura Lawton	7–8–9. Received cash on account from Laura Lawton, less sales discount and less sales tax. (p. 495)	7. _____	8. _____	9. _____
D. Sam Layton	10–11–12. Granted credit to Sam Layton for merchandise returned, plus sales tax. (p. 500)	10. _____	11. _____	12. _____
E. Purchases	13–14–15. Discovered that a sale on account to Laura Lawton was incorrectly charged to the account of Sam Layton. (p. 501)	13. _____	14. _____	15. _____
F. Purchases Discount	16–17–18. Recorded international cash sale. (p. 506)	16. _____	17. _____	18. _____
G. Purchases Returns and Allowances	19–20–21. Received a 60-day time draft from Bass Products, Inc., for an international sale. (p. 507)	19. _____	20. _____	21. _____
H. Sales	22–23–24. Received cash for the value of time draft. (p. 508)	22. _____	23. _____	24. _____
I. Sales Discount				
J. Sales Returns and Allowances				
K. Sales Tax Payable				
L. Time Drafts Receivable				

Part Three—Analyzing Sales and Cash Receipts

Directions: Place a *T* for True or an *F* for False in the Answers column to show whether each of the following statements is true or false.

Answers

1. All sales of merchandise on account are recorded in a sales journal. (p. 488)

   1. _____

2. Regardless of when merchandise is sold, revenue should be recorded when cash is received. (p. 488)

   2. _____

3. In some states, certain customers do not have to pay sales tax. (p. 489)

   3. _____

4. A sales invoice is the source document for journalizing a sales on account transaction. (p. 489)

   4. _____

5. When state regulations require that sales tax be paid only on actual sales realized, the reduction in sales tax is calculated by multiplying the original sales invoice amount by the sales discount rate. (p. 494)

   5. _____

6. When a customer receives credit terms of 1/10, n/30, the sales invoice amount is reduced 10% if the amount owed is paid within ten days. (p. 494)

   6. _____

7. Because Sales Discount is a contra account to Sales, it has a normal credit balance. (p. 495)

   7. _____

8. Sales discounts are recorded as a debit to Sales. (p. 495)

   8. _____

9. Sales returns and allowances always reduce revenue. (p. 499)

   9. _____

10. The best order to post special journals is (1) sales, (2) purchases, (3) general, (4) cash receipts, and (5) cash payments. (p. 502)

    10. _____

Study Guide 20

Name	Perfect Score	Your Score
Analyzing Uncollectible Accts. Expense and Allowance for Uncollectible Accts.	20 Pts.	
Analyzing Uncollectible Accounts Receivable	8 Pts.	
Journalizing Adjustments for Uncollectible Accounts Expense	12 Pts.	
Total	40 Pts.	

Part One—Analyzing Uncollectible Accounts Expense and Allowance for Uncollectible Accounts

Directions: Place a *T* for True or an *F* for False in the Answers column to show whether each of the following statements is true or false.

Answers

1. A business generally sells on account to encourage sales. (p. 524)

1. _____

2. Accounts receivable that cannot be collected are called uncollectible accounts. (p. 524)

2. _____

3. The amount of accounts receivable that is uncollectible decreases revenue. (p. 524)

3. _____

4. The Realization of Revenue accounting concept explains why failing to collect an account at a later date than the original sale cancels the sale and reduces revenue. (p. 524)

4. _____

5. A business usually knows at the time sales are made which customer accounts will become uncollectible. (p. 526)

5. _____

6. Allowances for Uncollectible Accounts is a contra account to its related asset account, Accounts Receivable. (p. 526)

6. _____

7. Crediting the estimated value of uncollectible accounts to a contra account is called the allowance method of recording losses from uncollectible accounts. (p. 526)

7. _____

8. The difference between an asset's account balance and its related contra account balance is called its book value. (p. 526)

8. _____

9. The difference between the balance of Accounts Receivable and its contra account, Allowance for Uncollectible Accounts, is called book value. (p. 526)

9. _____

10. Risk of loss occurs when a business sells on account. (p. 527)

10. _____

11. Estimating the percentage of uncollectible accounts expense in the same period as the sales revenue is an application of the Realization of Revenue accounting concept. (p. 527)

11. _____

12. The balance of the account Allowance for Uncollectible Accounts is extended to the Income Statement Credit column of the work sheet. (p. 528)

12. _____

13. When an adjusting entry for uncollectible accounts expense is recorded, Allowance for Uncollectible Accounts is credited. (p. 528)

13. _____

14. Using the percentage of total sales on account to estimate uncollectible accounts expense assumes that a portion of every sale on account dollar will become uncollectible. (p. 528)

14. _____

15. Canceling the balance of a customer account because the customer does not pay is called writing off an account. (p. 531)

15. _____

16. Allowance for Uncollectible Accounts is debited to write off a customer account. (p. 531)

16. _____

17. Accounts Receivable is debited to write off a customer account. (p. 531)

17. _____

18. When a customer account is written off under the allowance method, book value of accounts receivable decreases. (p. 531)

18. _____

19. When an account is written off, the account balance is transferred to Allowance for Uncollectible Accounts. (p. 531)

19. _____

20. When a previously written-off account is collected, Accounts Receivable is both debited and credited for the amount collected. (p. 533)

20. _____

Part Two—Analyzing Uncollectible Accounts Receivable

Directions: For each of the following items, select the choice that best completes the statement. Print the letter identifying your choice in the Answers column.

1. The loss from an uncollectible account is (A) a liability (B) a regular expense of doing business (C) an asset (D) a reduction in revenue. (p. 524)

   1. _____

2. Balance of accounts receivable less allowance for uncollectible accounts is the equation for calculating (A) uncollectible accounts expense (B) book value of accounts receivable (C) the contra account balance to accounts receivable (D) total collections of previously written-off accounts. (p. 526)

   2. _____

3. When the percentage of total sales on account method is used, the estimated uncollectible accounts expense is calculated by (A) multiplying total sales on account times the percentage (B) dividing total sales on account by the percentage (C) multiplying total sales times the percentage (D) dividing total sales by the percentage. (p. 527)

   3. _____

4. At the end of a fiscal period, the account debited to show the estimated amount of uncollectible accounts is (A) Accounts Receivable (B) Cash (C) Uncollectible Accounts Expense (D) Allowance for Uncollectible Accounts. (p. 528)

   4. _____

5. At the end of a fiscal period, the account credited to show the estimated amount of uncollectible accounts is (A) Cash (B) Uncollectible Accounts Expense (C) Accounts Receivable (D) Allowance for Uncollectible Accounts. (p. 528)

   5. _____

6. An Allowance for Uncollectible Accounts balance in the Trial Balance Credit column of a work sheet means (A) there are no uncollectible accounts (B) the estimate has not yet been recorded (C) previous fiscal period estimates have not yet been identified as uncollectible (D) equity has been maintained. (p. 528)

   6. _____

7. When the allowance account in the Trial Balance column of a work sheet has a credit balance, the amount of the adjustment is (A) deducted from the trial balance amount (B) not recorded (C) estimated (D) added to the Trial Balance amount. (p. 528)

   7. _____

8. When the account Allowance for Uncollectible Accounts is used, a customer past-due account is written off as uncollectible by (A) debiting Uncollectible Accounts Expense and crediting Accounts Receivable and the customer account (B) debiting Allowance for Uncollectible Accounts and crediting Accounts Receivable and the customer account (C) debiting Accounts Receivable and the customer account and crediting Allowance for Uncollectible Accounts (D) none of these. (p. 531)

   8. _____

Part Three—Journalizing Adjustments for Uncollectible Accounts Expense

Directions: In Answers Column l, print the abbreviation for the journal in which each transaction is to be recorded. In Answers Columns 2 and 3, print the letters identifying the accounts to be debited and credited for each transaction.

G—General journal   CR—Cash receipts journal

Account Title	Transaction	Journal	Answers Debit	Credit
A. Accounts Receivable	1–2–3. Recorded adjusting entry for uncollectible accounts expense. (p. 528)	1. _____	2. _____	3. _____
B. Allowance for Uncollectible Accounts	4–5–6. Wrote off Roger's Sports past-due account as uncollectible. (p. 531)	4. _____	5. _____	6. _____
C. Cash	Received cash in full payment of Roger's Sports account, previously written off as uncollectible:			
D. Roger's Sports	7–8–9. First entry. (p. 533)	7. _____	8. _____	9. _____
E. Uncollectible Accounts Expense	10–11–12. Second entry. (p. 534)	10. _____	11. _____	12. _____

Name	Perfect Score	Your Score
Analyzing Uncollectible Accts. Expense and Allowance for Uncollectible Accts.	14 Pts.	
Analyzing Plant Asset Transactions	14 Pts.	
Analyzing Plant Assets and Depreciation	10 Pts.	
Total	38 Pts.	

Part One—Analyzing Uncollectible Accounts Expense and Allowance for Uncollectible Accounts

Directions: Select the term in Column I that best fits each definition in Column II. Print the letter identifying your choice in the Answers column.

Column I	Column II	Answers
A. accumulated depreciation	1. Cash and other assets expected to be exchanged for cash or consumed within a year. (p. 544)	1. _____
B. assessed value	2. Assets that will be used for a number of years in the operation of a business. (p. 544)	2. _____
C. book value of a plant asset	3. Land and anything attached to the land. (p. 547)	3. _____
D. current assets	4. All property not classified as real property. (p. 547)	4. _____
E. declining-balance method of depreciation	5. The value of an asset determined by tax authorities for the purpose of calculating taxes. (p. 547)	5. _____
F. depreciation expense	6. The portion of a plant asset's cost that is transferred to an expense account in each fiscal period during a plant asset's useful life. (p. 549)	6. _____
G. estimated salvage value	7. The amount an owner expects to receive when a plant asset is removed from use. (p. 549)	7. _____
H. gain on plant assets	8. Charging an equal amount of depreciation expense for a plant asset in each year of useful life. (p. 550)	8. _____
I. loss on plant assets	9. The total amount of depreciation expense that has been recorded since the purchase of a plant asset. (p. 551)	9. _____
J. personal property	10. The original cost of a plant asset minus accumulated depreciation. (p. 551)	10. _____
K. plant asset record	11. An accounting form on which a business records information about each plant asset. (p. 553)	11. _____
L. plant assets	12. Revenue that results when a plant asset is sold for more than book value. (p. 559)	12. _____
M. real property	13. The loss that results when a plant asset is sold for less than book value. (p. 560)	13. _____
N. straight-line method of depreciation	14. Multiplying the book value by a constant depreciation rate at the end of each fiscal period. (p. 562)	14. _____

Part Two—Analyzing Plant Asset Transactions

Directions: Analyze each of the following transactions into debit and credit parts. Print the letter identifying your choices in the proper Answers column.

Account Title	Transaction	Answers Debit	Credit
A. Accumulated Depreciation—Office Equipment	1–2. Paid cash for new display case. (p. 546)	1. _____	2. _____
B. Accumulated Depreciation—Store Equipment	3–4. Paid cash for property taxes. (p. 547)	3. _____	4. _____
C. Cash	5–6. Recorded annual store equipment depreciation. (p. 554)	5. _____	6. _____
D. Depreciation Expense—Office Equipment	7–8. Received cash from sale of display case for book value. (p. 557)	7. _____	8. _____
E. Depreciation Expense—Store Equipment	9–10. Recorded a partial year's depreciation on a cash register to be sold. (p. 558)	9. _____	10. _____
F. Gain on Plant Assets	11–12. Received cash from sale of cash register for more than book value. (p. 559)	11. _____	12. _____
G. Office Equipment	13–14. Received cash from sale of a computer for less than book value. (p. 560)	13. _____	14. _____
H. Loss on Plant Assets			
I. Property Tax Expense			
J. Store Equipment			

Part Three—Analyzing Plant Assets and Depreciation

Directions: For each of the following items, select the choice that best completes the statement. Print the letter identifying your choice in the Answers column.

Answers

1. Recording a plant asset at its original cost is an application of the concept (A) Going Concern (B) Matching Expenses with Revenue (C) Objective Evidence (D) Historical Cost. (p. 546)

1. _____

2. A business buys plant assets (A) to use in earning revenue (B) to use as an investment (C) to sell for a profit (D) for employees' personal use. (p. 549)

2. _____

3. The amount by which a plant asset depreciates is classified as (A) revenue (B) a liability (C) an expense (D) an asset. (p. 549)

3. _____

4. Depreciation expense for a plant asset is recorded (A) when the asset is bought (B) after the asset is sold (C) when the asset is repaired (D) at the end of each fiscal period during the asset's estimated useful life. (p. 549)

4. _____

5. The smallest unit of time used to calculate depreciation is (A) one month (B) half a year (C) one year (D) none of these. (p. 550)

5. _____

6. The annual depreciation for a plant asset with original cost of $1,000.00, estimated salvage value of $100.00, and estimated useful life of 10 years, using the straight-line method, is (A) $100.00 (B) $1,000.00 (C) $900.00 (D) $90.00. (p. 550)

6. _____

7. The accumulated depreciation account should show (A) total depreciation for plant assets since the business was formed (B) total depreciation for plant assets still in use (C) only total depreciation expense for plant assets for the current year (D) next year's estimated depreciation for plant assets. (p. 551)

7. _____

8. When a plant asset is sold for the asset's book value, (A) cash received plus accumulated depreciation equals original cost (B) cash received plus salvage value equals original cost (C) cash received plus accumulated depreciation plus salvage value equals original cost (D) none of these. (p. 557)

8. _____

9. When a plant asset is sold for more than the asset's book value, (A) cash received plus accumulated depreciation plus gain on disposal equals original cost plus gain on disposal (B) cash received plus accumulated depreciation equals original cost plus gain on disposal (C) cash received plus accumulated depreciation plus loss on disposal equals original cost (D) cash received plus accumulated depreciation equals original cost plus loss on disposal. (p. 559)

9. _____

10. When a plant asset is sold for less than the asset's book value, (A) cash received plus accumulated depreciation plus gain on disposal equals original cost (B) cash received plus accumulated depreciation plus loss on disposal equals original cost (C) cash received plus accumulated depreciation equals original cost plus gain on disposal (D) cash received plus accumulated depreciation equals original cost plus loss on disposal. (p. 560)

10. _____

Study Guide 22

Part One—Identifying Accounting Terms

Directions: Select the one term in Column I that best fits each definition in Column II. Print the letter identifying your choice in the Answers column.

Column I	Column II	Answers
A. first-in, first-out inventory costing method	1. A merchandise inventory determined by counting, weighing, or measuring items of merchandise on hand. (p. 574)	1. _____
B. gross profit method of estimating inventory	2. A merchandise inventory determined by keeping a continuous record of increases, decreases, and balance on hand. (p. 574)	2. _____
C. inventory record	3. A form used during a periodic inventory to record information about each item of merchandise on hand. (p. 575)	3. _____
D. last-in, first-out inventory costing method	4. A form used to show the kind of merchandise, quantity received, quantity sold, and balance on hand. (p. 576)	4. _____
E. periodic inventory	5. A file of stock records for all merchandise on hand. (p. 576)	5. _____
F. perpetual inventory	6. Using the price of merchandise purchased first to calculate the cost of merchandise sold first. (p. 578)	6. _____
G. stock ledger	7. Using the price of merchandise purchased last to calculate the cost of merchandise sold first. (p. 579)	7. _____
H. stock record	8. Using the average cost of beginning inventory plus merchandise purchased during a fiscal period to calculate the cost of merchandise sold. (p. 580)	8. _____
I. weighted-average inventory costing method	9. Estimating inventory by using the previous year's percentage of gross profit on operations. (p. 583)	9. _____

Part Two—Analyzing Inventory Systems

Directions: Place a *T* for True or an *F* for False in the Answers column to show whether each of the following statements is true or false.

Answers

1. Merchandise inventory on hand is typically the largest asset of a merchandising business. (p. 572)

1. _____

2. The only financial statement on which the value of merchandise on hand is reported is the income statement. (p. 572)

2. _____

3. Net income of a business can be decreased by maintaining a merchandise inventory that is larger than needed. (p. 574)

3. _____

4. A perpetual inventory is sometimes known as a physical inventory. (p. 574)

4. _____

5. A minimum inventory balance is the amount of merchandise that will typically last until ordered merchandise can be received from vendors. (p. 576)

5. _____

6. A periodic inventory should be taken at least once a month, even when perpetual inventory records are kept. (p. 575)

6. _____

7. A perpetual inventory system provides day-to-day information about the quality of merchandise on hand. (p. 576)

7. _____

8. Some cash registers use optical scanners to read the UPC codes marked on products. (p. 576)

8. _____

9. First-in, first-out is a method used to determine the quantity of each type of merchandise on hand. (p. 578)

9. _____

10. The gross profit method makes it possible to prepare monthly income statements without taking a periodic inventory. (p. 583)

10. _____

Part Three—Analyzing Lifo, Fifo, and Weighted-Average Methods

Directions: For each of the following items, select the choice that best completes the statement. Print the letter identifying your choice in the Answers column.

Answers

1. Calculating an accurate inventory cost to assure that gross profit and net income are reported correctly on the income statement is an application of the accounting concept (A) Consistent Reporting (B) Perpetual Inventory (C) Adequate Disclosure (D) none of these. (p. 572)

   1. _____

2. The fifo method is based on the assumption that the merchandise purchased first is the merchandise (A) sold first (B) sold last (C) in beginning inventory (D) none of these. (p. 578)

   2. _____

3. When the fifo method is used, cost of merchandise sold is valued at the (A) average price (B) most recent price (C) earliest price (D) none of these. (p. 578)

   3. _____

4. When the fifo method is used, ending inventory units are priced at the (A) average price (B) earliest price (C) most recent price (D) none of these. (p. 578)

   4. _____

5. Using an inventory costing method that charges the most recent costs of merchandise against current revenue is an application of the accounting concept (A) Adequate Disclosure (B) Consistent Reporting (C) Matching Expenses with Revenue (D) none of these. (p. 579)

   5. _____

6. The lifo method is based on the assumption that the merchandise purchased last is the merchandise (A) sold first (B) sold last (C) in ending inventory (D) none of these. (p. 579)

   6. _____

7. When the lifo method is used, cost of merchandise sold is priced at the (A) average price (B) earliest price (C) most recent price (D) none of these. (p. 579)

   7. _____

8. The weighted-average method is based on the assumption that the cost of merchandise sold should be calculated using the (A) average price per unit of beginning inventory (B) average price of ending inventory (C) average price of beginning inventory plus purchases during the fiscal period (D) average price of ending inventory plus purchases during the fiscal period. (p. 580)

   8. _____

9. When the weighted-average method is used, ending inventory units are priced at the (A) earliest price (B) most recent price (C) average price (D) none of these. (p. 580)

   9. _____

10. A business that uses the same inventory costing method for all fiscal periods is applying the accounting concept (A) Consistent Reporting (B) Accounting Period Cycle (C) Perpetual Inventory (D) Adequate Disclosure. (p. 581)

    10. _____

11. In a year of falling prices, the inventory method that gives the lowest possible value for ending inventory is (A) weighted-average (B) lifo (C) fifo (D) gross profit. (p. 581)

    11. _____

(Continued)

12. Inventory information for Johnson Company is shown below:

	Units	Unit Price
Beginning inventory	20	$20.00
Purchases during the year	40	$30.00
Ending inventory	30	

Under the fifo method, ending inventory is (A) $900.00 (B) $750.00 (C) $700.00 (D) none of these. (p. 581)

13. In a year of rising prices, the inventory method that gives the lowest possible value for ending inventory is (A) fifo (B) lifo (C) weighted-average (D) gross profit. (p. 581)

14. Using the inventory information in Question 12, ending inventory under the lifo method is (A) $900.00 (B) $750.00 (C) $700.00 (D) none of these. (p. 581)

15. Using the inventory information in Question 12, ending inventory under the weighted-average method is (A) $900.00 (B) $750.00 (C) $700.00 (D) none of these. (p. 580)

Study Guide 23

Name	Perfect Score	Your Score
Identifying Accounting Terms	18 Pts.	
Identifying Accounting Concepts and Practices	8 Pts.	
Analyzing Notes Payable and Notes Receivable Transactions	14 Pts.	
Analyzing Notes and Interest	10 Pts.	
Total	50 Pts.	

Part One—Identifying Accounting Terms

Directions: Select the one term in Column I that best fits each definition in Column II. Print the letter identifying your choice in the Answers column.

Column I	Column II	Answers
A. creditor	1. The number assigned to identify a specific note. (p. 594)	1. _____
B. current liabilities	2. The date a note is signed. (p. 594)	2. _____
C. date of a note	3. The person or business to whom the amount of a note is payable. (p. 594)	3. _____
D. dishonored note	4. The days, months, or years from the date of signing until a note is to be paid. (p. 594)	4. _____
E. interest	5. The original amount of a note. (p. 594)	5. _____
F. interest expense	6. The percentage of the principal that is paid for use of the money. (p. 594)	6. _____
G. interest income	7. The date a note is due. (p. 594)	7. _____
H. interest rate of a note	8. The person or business who signs a note and thus promises to make payment. (p. 594)	8. _____
I. maker of a note	9. A written and signed promise to pay a sum of money at a specified time. (p. 594)	9. _____
J. maturity date of a note	10. A person or organization to whom a liability is owed. (p. 594)	10. _____
K. maturity value	11. Promissory notes signed by a business and given to a creditor. (p. 594)	11. _____
L. notes payable	12. An amount paid for the use of money for a period of time. (p. 595)	12. _____
M. notes receivable	13. The amount that is due on the maturity date of a note. (p. 595)	13. _____
N. number of a note	14. Liabilities due within a short time, usually within a year. (p. 598)	14. _____
O. payee of a note	15. The interest accrued on money borrowed. (p. 599)	15. _____
P. principal of a note	16. Promissory notes that a business accepts from customers. (p. 603)	16. _____
Q. promissory note	17. The interest earned on money loaned. (p. 604)	17. _____
R. time of a note	18. A note that is not paid when due. (p. 605)	18. _____

Part Two—Identifying Accounting Concepts and Practices

Directions: Place a *T* for True or an *F* for False in the Answers column to show whether each of the following statements is true or false.

Answers

1. When the timing of cash receipts and required cash payments do not match, businesses usually deposit extra cash or borrow cash or make arrangements to delay payments. (p. 592)

   1. _____

2. "Interest at 12%" means that 12 cents will be paid for the use of each dollar borrowed for the time of a note. (p. 595)

   2. _____

3. An individual with a car loan usually pays the note in partial payments that include part of the principal and part of the interest on the note. (p. 595)

   3. _____

4. In interest calculations, time can be expressed in whole years or as a fraction of a year. (p. 595)

   4. _____

5. The maturity value of a note is calculated by subtracting the interest rate from the principal. (p. 595)

   5. _____

6. The journal entry for signing a note payable includes a debit to Interest Expense. (p. 598)

   6. _____

7. The journal entry for paying a note payable includes a debit to Accounts Payable to remove the balance owed. (p. 601)

   7. _____

8. When a note receivable is dishonored, the company should immediately write off the account receivable for that customer. (p. 605)

   8. _____

Part Three—Analyzing Notes Payable and Notes Receivable Transactions

Directions: Analyze each of the following transactions into debit and credit parts. Print the letter identifying your choices in the proper Answers column.

Account Titles	Transactions	Answers Debit	Credit
A. Accounts Payable	1–2. Signed a 90-day, 10% note. (p. 598)	1. _____	2. _____
B. Accounts Receivable	3–4. Paid cash for the maturity value of a note plus interest. (p. 599)	3. _____	4. _____
C. Cash	5–6. Signed a 60-day, 18% note to Classy Plants for an extension of time on an account payable. (p. 600)	5. _____	6. _____
D. Interest Expense	7–8. Paid cash for the maturity value of the note payable to Classy Plants. (p. 601)	7. _____	8. _____
E. Interest Income	9–10. Accepted a 90-day, 18% note from Bette David for an extension of time on her account. (p. 603)	9. _____	10. _____
F. Notes Payable	11–12. Received cash for the maturity value of the note receivable plus interest from Bette David. (p. 604)	11. _____	12. _____
G. Notes Receivable	13–14. Martin's Plants dishonored a note receivable, maturity value due today. (p. 605)	13. _____	14. _____

ACCTS. RECEIVABLE LEDGER

H. Bette David

I. Martin's Plants

ACCTS. PAYABLE LEDGER

J. Classy Plants

Part Four—Analyzing Notes and Interest

Directions: For each of the following items, select the choice that best completes the statement. Print the letter identifying your choice in the Answers column.

1. The most useful evidence of a debt in a court of law is (A) an oral promise to pay (B) an account receivable (C) an account payable (D) a signed note. (p. 594)

   1. _____

2. The time of a note issued for less than one year is typically stated in (A) days (B) months (C) a fraction of a year (D) none of these. (p. 595)

   2. _____

3. The interest on a 180-day, 10% interest-bearing note of $2,000.00 is (A) $20.00 (B) $200.00 (C) $100.00 (D) none of these. (p. 595)

   3. _____

4. The maturity value of a 90-day, 12% interest-bearing note of $600.00 is (A) $582.00 (B) $672.00 (C) $624.00 (D) none of these. (p. 595)

   4. _____

5. The maturity date of a 90-day note dated August 22 is (A) November 19 (B) November 20 (C) November 21 (D) November 22. (p. 596)

   5. _____

6. Notes payable are classified as (A) current assets (B) current liabilities (C) expenses (D) revenue. (p. 598)

   6. _____

7. The source document for recording cash received from signing a note payable is a (A) receipt (B) check (C) memorandum (D) copy of the note. (p. 598)

   7. _____

8. Interest expense of a business is (A) an additional cost of merchandise (B) a normal operations expense (C) a financial expense (D) a contra revenue account. (p. 599)

   8. _____

9. When a business accepts a note from a customer for an extension of time on account, the customer's accounts receivable account is (A) not affected (B) changed to a zero balance (C) equal to the principal plus interest of the note (D) debited for the amount of the note. (p. 600)

   9. _____

10. Notes receivable are classified as (A) other expense (B) current assets (C) current liabilities (D) other revenue. (p. 603)

    10. _____

Study Guide 24

Name		Perfect Score	Your Score
	Identifying Accounting Concepts and Practices	15 Pts.	
	Analyzing Accounts Affected by Accrued Revenue and Accrued Expenses	18 Pts.	
	Analyzing Accrued Revenue and Accrued Expenses	12 Pts.	
	Total	45 Pts.	

Part One—Identifying Accounting Concepts and Practices

Directions: For each of the following items, select the choice that best completes the statement. Print the letter identifying your choice in the Answers column.

Answers

1. Revenue earned in one fiscal period but not received until a later fiscal period is called (A) accrued expense (B) accrued interest expense (C) accrued revenue (D) accrued interest income. (p. 614)

1. _____

2. At the end of a fiscal period, each expense that has been incurred but not paid should be recorded as (A) an adjusting entry (B) a reversing entry (C) a closing entry (D) an opening entry. (p. 614)

2. _____

3. Recording adjusting entries for the fiscal period in which the revenue has been earned regardless of when it will be received is an application of the accounting concept (A) Objective Evidence (B) Realization of Revenue (C) Adequate Disclosure (D) Historical Cost. (p. 614)

3. _____

4. Interest earned but not yet received is called (A) accrued interest income (B) interest income (C) earned income (D) none of these. (p. 616)

4. _____

5. At the end of a fiscal period, any revenue that has been earned but not received should be credited to an appropriate (A) revenue account (B) expense account (C) liability account (D) asset account. (p. 616)

5. _____

6. Interest Receivable is (A) an asset (B) a liability (C) revenue (D) an expense. (p. 617)

6. _____

7. An entry made at the beginning of one fiscal period to reverse an adjusting entry made in the previous fiscal period is called (A) a debit entry (B) a credit entry (C) a reversing entry (D) none of these. (p. 618)

7. _____

8. A reversing entry for accrued interest income results in a debit to (A) Interest Receivable (B) Notes Receivable (C) Income Summary (D) Interest Income. (p. 618)

8. _____

9. A reversing entry for accrued interest income will result in an account balance of (A) Interest Receivable Debit (B) Interest Income Debit (C) Interest Receivable Credit (D) Interest Income Credit. (p. 618)

9. _____

10. Expenses incurred in one fiscal period but not paid until a later fiscal period are called (A) accrued interest expenses (B) accrued expenses (C) accrued income expenses (D) accrued interest receivable. (p. 621)

10. _____

11. Interest incurred but not yet paid is called (A) accrued income expense (B) earned income (C) accrued interest expense (D) interest expense. (p. 621)

11. _____

12. At the end of a fiscal period, each expense that has been incurred but not paid should be debited to an appropriate (A) revenue account (B) expense account (C) asset account (D) liability account. (p. 621)

12. _____

13. At the end of a fiscal period, each expense that has been incurred but not paid should be credited to an appropriate (A) revenue account (B) expense account (C) asset account (D) liability account. (p. 621)

13. _____

14. A reversing entry for accrued interest expense will result in an account balance of (A) Interest Payable Debit (B) Interest Payable Credit (C) Interest Expense Debit (D) Interest Expense Credit. (p. 623)

14. _____

15. An adjusting entry normally is reversed if the adjusting entry creates a balance in (A) a revenue or expense account (B) a revenue and liability account (C) an expense and asset account (D) an asset or liability account. (p. 625)

15. _____

Part Two—Analyzing Accounts Affected by Accrued Revenue and Accrued Expenses

Directions: Analyze each of the following entries into debit and credit parts. Print the letter identifying your choice in the proper Answers columns. Determine in which journal each of the transactions are to be recorded.

G—General Journal   CP—Cash Payments Journal   CR—Cash Receipts Journal

Account Titles	Transactions	Journal	Answers Debit	Credit
A. Cash	1–2–3. Recorded an adjustment for accrued interest income. (p. 616)	1. _____	2. _____	3. _____
B. Interest Expense	4–5–6. Reversed an adjusting entry for accrued interest income. (p. 618)	4. _____	5. _____	6. _____
C. Interest Income	7–8–9. Received cash for the maturity value of a 90-day, 12% note. (p. 619)	7. _____	8. _____	9. _____
D. Interest Payable	10–11–12. Recorded an adjustment for accrued interest expense. (p. 621)	10. _____	11. _____	12. _____
E. Interest Receivable	13–14–15. Reversed an adjusting entry for accrued interest expense. (p. 623)	13. _____	14. _____	15. _____
F. Notes Payable	16–17–18. Paid cash for the maturity value of a previous note payable. (p. 624)	16. _____	17. _____	18. _____
G. Notes Receivable				

Part Three—Analyzing Accrued Revenue and Accrued Expenses

Directions: Place a *T* for True or an *F* for False in the Answers column to show whether each of the following statements is true or false.

Answers

1. Reporting all liabilities on a balance sheet, including accrued expenses, is an application of the accounting concept Matching Expenses with Revenue. (p. 614)

    1. _____

2. Revenue should be recorded when the revenue is earned. (p. 614)

    2. _____

3. Adjusting entries are made at the beginning of each fiscal period. (p. 614)

    3. _____

4. The adjustment for accrued interest income is planned on a work sheet. (p. 616)

    4. _____

5. Accrued interest income is credited to the interest income account. (p. 616)

    5. _____

6. When an adjusting entry for accrued interest income is made, Interest Receivable is debited. (p. 616)

    6. _____

7. Accrued interest is calculated by multiplying principal times interest rate times time as a fraction of a year. (p. 616)

    7. _____

8. A reversing entry for interest income reduces the balance of Interest Receivable. (p. 618)

    8. _____

9. Reversing entries are made on the last day of the fiscal period. (p. 618)

    9. _____

10. At the end of a fiscal period, the Interest Expense balance after adjustments shows the amount of interest expense that has been incurred in that fiscal period. (p. 621)

    10. _____

11. An Interest Payable credit balance is accrued interest expense incurred in the current year but to be paid in the next year. (p. 621)

    11. _____

12. When a reversing entry is made for accrued interest expense, a debit entry is required to Interest Payable. (p. 623)

    12. _____

Study Guide 25

Name	Perfect Score	Your Score
Identifying Accounting Concepts and Practices	26 Pts.	
Analyzing Dividend Transactions and Adjusting Entries for a Corporation	24 Pts.	
Total	50 Pts.	

Part One—Identifying Accounting Concepts and Practices

Directions: Place a *T* for True or an *F* for False in the Answers column to show whether each of the following statements is true or false.

Answers

1. A stockholder is an owner of one or more shares of a corporation. (p. 636) 1. _____
2. Owners' equity accounts for a corporation normally are listed under a major chart of accounts division titled Operating Expenses. (p. 636) 2. _____
3. A dividend is an amount earned by a corporation and not yet distributed to stockholders. (p. 636) 3. _____
4. Retained earnings are earnings distributed to stockholders. (p. 636) 4. _____
5. Separate general ledger accounts are kept for each owner of a corporation. (p. 636) 5. _____
6. A dividends account has a normal debit balance and is increased by a debit. (p. 637) 6. _____
7. A group of persons elected by the stockholders to manage a corporation is called a board of directors. (p. 637) 7. _____
8. A board of directors distributes earnings of a corporation to stockholders by declaring a dividend. (p. 637) 8. _____
9. A corporation does not need to pay a declared dividend if it does not have enough cash to do so. (p. 637) 9. _____
10. A check is the source document for declaring a dividend. (p. 637) 10. _____
11. The accounts used to record the declaration of a dividend are Dividends Payable and Dividends Expense. (p. 637) 11. _____
12. A declared dividend is classified as an expense. (p. 637) 12. _____
13. When a declared dividend is paid, Dividends Payable is debited. (p. 638) 13. _____
14. Work sheet adjustments for interest expense are made for corporations but not for proprietorships. (p. 640) 14. _____
15. Work sheets for corporations, proprietorships, and partnerships are similar. (p. 640) 15. _____
16. The two accounts used to make an uncollectible accounts expense adjustment are Uncollectible Accounts Expense and Allowance for Uncollectible Accounts. (p. 641) 16. _____
17. Federal income tax is an expense of a corporation. (p. 646) 17. _____
18. When a corporation makes the quarterly payment of estimated federal income tax, Federal Income Tax Payable is credited. (p. 646) 18. _____
19. The balance of Federal Income Tax Expense in the Trial Balance columns of the work sheet is the amount of income tax paid in quarterly installments. (p. 648) 19. _____
20. The amount extended to the Federal Income Tax Payable Balance Sheet column is the amount of federal income tax still to be paid by the corporation. (p. 646) 20. _____
21. Federal income tax is calculated by multiplying net sales by the tax rate. (p. 646) 21. _____
22. The first step in calculating federal income tax is to extend all work sheet amounts to the Income Statement and Balance Sheet columns. (p. 646) 22. _____
23. Corporations with less than $50,000 net income pay smaller tax rates than corporations with larger net incomes. (p. 647) 23. _____
24. When the total of a work sheet's Income Statement Credit column is larger than the total of the Income Statement Debit column, the difference represents net loss of the business. (p. 649) 24. _____
25. A work sheet's Balance Sheet columns are used to calculate net income after federal income tax. (p. 649) 25. _____
26. The balance of Capital Stock is recorded in the Income Statement columns of a work sheet. (p. 650) 26. _____

Part Two—Analyzing Dividend Transactions and Adjusting Entries for a Corporation

Directions: Analyze each of the following transactions into debit and credit parts. Print the letter identifying the accounts debited and credited in the proper Answers columns.

Account Titles	Transactions	Answers Debit	Credit
A. Accumulated Depreciation—Office Equipment	1–2. Declared stockholders' dividend. (p. 637)	1. _____	2. _____
B. Accumulated Depreciation—Store Equipment	3–4. Paid cash for dividends declared. (p. 638)	3. _____	4. _____
C. Allowance for Uncollectible Accounts	5–6. Adjusting entry for accrued interest income. (p. 641)	5. _____	6. _____
D. Cash	7–8. Adjusting entry for uncollectible accounts expense. (p. 641)	7. _____	8. _____
E. Depreciation Expense—Office Equipment	9–10. Adjusting entry for a decrease in merchandise inventory. (p. 642)	9. _____	10. _____
F. Depreciation Expense—Store Equipment	11–12. Adjusting entry for an increase in merchandise inventory. (p. 642)	11. _____	12. _____
G. Dividends	13–14. Adjusting entry for supplies. (p. 643)	13. _____	14. _____
H. Dividends Payable	15–16. Adjusting entry for prepaid insurance. (p. 643)	15. _____	16. _____
I. Federal Income Tax Expense	17–18. Adjusting entry for depreciation expense—store equipment. (p. 644)	17. _____	18. _____
J. Federal Income Tax Payable	19–20. Adjusting entry for depreciation expense—office equipment. (p. 644)	19. _____	20. _____
K. Income Summary	21–22. Adjusting entry for accrued interest expense. (p. 644)	21. _____	22. _____
L. Insurance Expense	23–24. Adjusting entry for federal income tax. (p. 648)	23. _____	24. _____
M. Interest Expense			
N. Interest Income			
O. Interest Payable			
P. Interest Receivable			
Q. Merchandise Inventory			
R. Prepaid Insurance			
S. Supplies			
T. Supplies Expense			
U. Uncollectible Accounts Expense			

Study Guide 26

Name		Perfect Score	Your Score
	Identifying Accounting Terms	8 Pts.	
	Analyzing End-of-Fiscal-Period Work for a Corporation	11 Pts.	
	Analyzing End-of-Fiscal-Period Entries for a Corporation	34 Pts.	
	Total	53 Pts.	

Part One—Identifying Accounting Terms

Directions: Select the one term in Column I that best fits each definition in Column II. Print the letter identifying your choice in the Answers column.

Column I	Column II	Answers
A. current ratio	1. Total sales less sales discount and sales returns and allowances. (p. 663)	1. _____
B. long-term liabilities	2. Total purchases less purchases discount and purchases returns and allowances. (p. 663)	2. _____
C. net purchases	3. A financial statement that shows changes in a corporation's ownership for a fiscal period. (p. 666)	3. _____
D. net sales	4. A value assigned to a share of stock and printed on the stock certificate. (p. 666)	4. _____
E. par value	5. Liabilities owed for more than a year. (p. 670)	5. _____
F. ratio	6. The amount of total current assets less total current liabilities. (p. 673)	6. _____
G. statement of stockholders' equity	7. A comparison between two numbers showing how many times one number exceeds the other. (p. 673)	7. _____
H. working capital	8. A ratio that shows the numeric relationship of current assets to current liabilities. (p. 673)	8. _____

Part Two—Analyzing End-of-Fiscal-Period Work for a Corporation

Directions: Place a *T* for True or an *F* for False in the Answers column to show whether each of the following statements is true or false.

1. A corporation's preparation of financial statements at the end of each year is an application of the Accounting Period Cycle concept. (p. 660)

   1. _____

2. Net purchases is reported in the Operating Expenses section of an income statement. (p. 662)

   2. _____

3. Net sales is reported in the Operating Revenue section of an income statement. (p. 662)

   3. _____

4. To calculate the component percentage of cost of merchandise sold, divide net sales by cost of merchandise sold. (p. 664)

   4. _____

5. A statement of stockholders' equity contains two major sections: capital stock and retained earnings. (p. 666)

   5. _____

6. A declared dividend is reported on the income statement as an expense. (p. 667)

   6. _____

7. An example of a long-term liability is Mortgage Payable. (p. 670)

   7. _____

8. The stockholders' equity section of a balance sheet contains accounts related to capital stock and earnings kept in the business. (p. 671)

   8. _____

9. A corporation's capital stock plus retained earnings always equals total assets. (p. 672)

   9. _____

10. Dividends decrease the earnings retained by a corporation. (p. 678)

    10. _____

11. A reversing entry is desirable if an adjusting entry creates a balance in an asset or a liability account. (p. 679)

    11. _____

Part Three—Analyzing End-of-Fiscal-Period Entries for a Corporation

Directions: For each closing or reversing entry described, decide which accounts are debited and credited. Print the letter identifying your choice in the proper Answers columns. (Accounts are listed in chart of accounts order.)

Account Titles	Closing/Reversing Entry	Answers Debit	Credit
A. Interest Receivable	1–2. Closing entry for the sales account. (p. 676)	1. _____	2. _____
B. Merchandise Inventory	3–4. Closing entry for purchases discount. (p. 676)	3. _____	4. _____
C. Supplies	5–6. Closing entry for the purchases returns and allowances account. (p. 676)	5. _____	6. _____
D. Prepaid Insurance	7–8. Closing entry for the gain on plant assets account. (p. 676)	7. _____	8. _____
E. Interest Payable	9–10. Closing entry for the interest income account. (p. 676)	9. _____	10. _____
F. Federal Income Tax Payable	11–12. Closing entry for the sales discount account. (p. 676)	11. _____	12. _____
G. Dividends Payable	13–14. Closing entry for the purchases account. (p. 677)	13. _____	14. _____
H. Retained Earnings	15–16. Closing entry for the cash short and over account (cash is short). (p. 677)	15. _____	16. _____
I. Dividends	17–18. Closing entry for the cash short and over account (cash is over). (p. 677)	17. _____	18. _____
J. Income Summary	19–20. Closing entry for the depreciation expense—store equipment account. (p. 677)	19. _____	20. _____
K. Sales	21–22. Closing entry for the federal income tax expense account. (p. 677)	21. _____	22. _____
L. Sales Discount	23–24. Closing entry for the income summary account (net income). (p. 678)	23. _____	24. _____
M. Purchases	25–26. Closing entry for the dividends account. (p. 678)	25. _____	26. _____
N. Purchases Discount	27–28. Closing entry for the income summary account (net loss). (p. 678)	27. _____	28. _____
O. Purchases Returns and Allowances	29–30. Reversing entry for the accrued interest income account. (p. 679)	29. _____	30. _____
P. Cash Short and Over	31–32. Reversing entry for the accrued interest expense. (p. 679)	31. _____	32. _____
Q. Depreciation Expense— Store Equipment	33–34. Reversing entry for the federal income tax payable account. (p. 679)	33. _____	34. _____

(Continued)

Account Titles

R. Insurance Expense

S. Supplies Expense

T. Uncollectible Accounts
Expense

U. Gain on Plant Assets

V. Interest Income

W. Interest Expense

X. Loss on Plant Assets

Y. Federal Income Tax Expense

1-1 RECYCLING PROBLEM, p. C-1

Determining how transactions change an accounting equation and preparing a balance sheet

1.

Trans. No.	Assets						=	Liabilities	+ Owner's Equity
	Cash	+	Supplies	+	Prepaid Insurance	=		Accts. Pay.— Divers Supply	Alston Eubanks, Capital
New Bal. 1.	0 +1,700		0		0			0	0 +1,700
New Bal. 2.	1,700		0		0			0	1,700
New Bal. 3.									
New Bal. 4.									
New Bal. 5.									
New Bal. 6.									
New Bal.									

2.

Trans. No.	Assets				=	Liabilities	+	Owner's Equity
	Cash	+	Supplies	+	Prepaid Insurance	=		+
New Bal. 1.								
New Bal. 2.								
New Bal. 3.								
New Bal. 4.								
New Bal. 5.								
New Bal. 6.								
New Bal.								

2-1 RECYCLING PROBLEM, p. C-2

Determining how transactions change an accounting equation and preparing a balance sheet

1.

Trans. No.	Cash	+	Accts. Rec.— Club Scuba	+ Supplies +	Prepaid Insurance =	Accts. Pay.— Divers Supply	+	Alston Eubanks, Capital
			Assets		=	Liabilities	+	Owner's Equity
Beg. Bal. 1.	1,195 −150		− 0 −	1,030	175	300		2,100 −150 (expense)
New Bal. 2.	1,045		− 0 −	1,030	175	300		1,950
New Bal. 3.								
New Bal. 4.								
New Bal. 5.								
New Bal. 6.								
New Bal. 7.								
New Bal. 8.								
New Bal. 9.								
New Bal. 10.								
New Bal. 11.								
New Bal. 12.								
New Bal. 13.								
New Bal.								

2.

Extra form

3-1 RECYCLING PROBLEM, p. C-3

Analyzing transactions into debit and credit parts

Extra forms

Extra form

JOURNAL

PAGE

DATE	ACCOUNT TITLE	DOC. NO.	POST. REF.	GENERAL DEBIT 1	GENERAL CREDIT 2	SALES CREDIT 3	CASH DEBIT 4	CASH CREDIT 5
1								
2								
3								
4								
5								
6								
7								
8								
9								
10								
11								
12								
13								
14								
15								
16								
17								
18								
19								
20								
21								
22								
23								
24								
25								

4-1 RECYCLING PROBLEM, p. C-4

Journalizing transactions and proving and ruling a journal

1., 2.

JOURNAL

PAGE 1

	DATE	ACCOUNT TITLE	DOC. NO.	POST. REF.	GENERAL DEBIT	GENERAL CREDIT	SALES CREDIT	CASH DEBIT	CASH CREDIT	
1										1
2										2
3										3
4										4
5										5
6										6
7										7
8										8
9										9
10										10
11										11
12										12
13										13
14										14
15										15
16										16
17										17
18										18
19										19
20										20
21										21
22										22
23										23
24										24
25										25

  CENTURY 21 ACCOUNTING, 7TH EDITION

4-1 **RECYCLING PROBLEM (concluded)**

2., 3., 6.

JOURNAL

PAGE 2

			1	2	3	4	5
DATE	ACCOUNT TITLE	DOC. NO.	POST. REF.	GENERAL		SALES CREDIT	CASH	
				DEBIT	CREDIT		DEBIT	CREDIT
1								
2								
3								
4								
5								
6								
7								
8								
9								
10								
11								
12								
13								
14								
15								

2. *Prove page 1 of the journal:*

	Debit	*Credit*
Column	*Column Totals*	*Column Totals*
General	_____	_____
Sales	_____	_____
Cash	_____	_____
Totals	_____	_____

4. *Prove page 2 of the journal:*

	Debit	*Credit*
Column	*Column Totals*	*Column Totals*
General	_____	_____
Sales	_____	_____
Cash	_____	_____
Totals	_____	_____

5. *Prove cash:*

Cash on hand at the beginning of the month . . . . _____
Plus total cash received during the month . . . . _____
Equals Total . . . . _____
Less total cash paid during the month . . . . _____
Equals cash balance at the end of the month . . . . _____
Checkbook balance on the next unused check stub . . . . . . _____

Extra form

JOURNAL

					GENERAL		SALES	CASH		
					1	2	3	4	5	
DATE	ACCOUNT TITLE	DOC. NO.	POST. REF.		DEBIT	CREDIT	SALES CREDIT	DEBIT	CREDIT	

Extra form

JOURNAL

PAGE

DATE	ACCOUNT TITLE	DOC. NO.	POST. REF.	GENERAL DEBIT 1	GENERAL CREDIT 2	SALES CREDIT 3	CASH DEBIT 4	CASH CREDIT 5

5-1 RECYCLING PROBLEM, p. C-5

Journalizing transactions and posting to a general ledger

2., 5., 6.

JOURNAL   PAGE 1

DATE	ACCOUNT TITLE	DOC. NO.	POST. REF.	GENERAL DEBIT	GENERAL CREDIT	SALES CREDIT	CASH DEBIT	CASH CREDIT	
									1
									2
									3
									4
									5
									6
									7
									8
									9
									10
									11
									12
									13
									14
									15
									16
									17
									18
									19
									20

3. *Prove the journal:*

Column	Debit Column Totals	Credit Column Totals
General	_____	_____
Sales	_____	_____
Cash	_____	_____
Totals	_____	_____

4. *Prove cash:*

Cash on hand at the beginning of the month . . . . _____
Plus total cash received during the month . . . . _____
Equals Total . . . . _____
Less total cash paid during the month . . . . _____
Equals cash balance at the end of the month . . . . _____
Checkbook balance on the next unused check stub . . . . _____

5-1 RECYCLING PROBLEM (continued)

1., 6.   **GENERAL LEDGER**

ACCOUNT Cash   ACCOUNT NO. 110

DATE	ITEM	POST. REF.	DEBIT	CREDIT	BALANCE DEBIT	BALANCE CREDIT

ACCOUNT Accounts Receivable—Nicholas Calendo   ACCOUNT NO. 120

DATE	ITEM	POST. REF.	DEBIT	CREDIT	BALANCE DEBIT	BALANCE CREDIT

ACCOUNT Supplies   ACCOUNT NO. 130

DATE	ITEM	POST. REF.	DEBIT	CREDIT	BALANCE DEBIT	BALANCE CREDIT

ACCOUNT Accounts Payable—Jordan Supplies   ACCOUNT NO. 210

DATE	ITEM	POST. REF.	DEBIT	CREDIT	BALANCE DEBIT	BALANCE CREDIT

ACCOUNT Janet Porter, Capital   ACCOUNT NO. 310

DATE	ITEM	POST. REF.	DEBIT	CREDIT	BALANCE DEBIT	BALANCE CREDIT

1., 6.   **GENERAL LEDGER**

ACCOUNT Janet Porter, Drawing   ACCOUNT NO. 320

DATE	ITEM	POST. REF.	DEBIT	CREDIT	BALANCE DEBIT	BALANCE CREDIT

ACCOUNT Sales   ACCOUNT NO. 410

DATE	ITEM	POST. REF.	DEBIT	CREDIT	BALANCE DEBIT	BALANCE CREDIT

ACCOUNT Advertising Expense   ACCOUNT NO. 510

DATE	ITEM	POST. REF.	DEBIT	CREDIT	BALANCE DEBIT	BALANCE CREDIT

ACCOUNT Miscellaneous Expense   ACCOUNT NO. 520

DATE	ITEM	POST. REF.	DEBIT	CREDIT	BALANCE DEBIT	BALANCE CREDIT

ACCOUNT Rent Expense   ACCOUNT NO. 530

DATE	ITEM	POST. REF.	DEBIT	CREDIT	BALANCE DEBIT	BALANCE CREDIT

ACCOUNT   ACCOUNT NO.

DATE	ITEM	POST. REF.	DEBIT	CREDIT	BALANCE DEBIT	BALANCE CREDIT

Name _____ Date _____ Class _____

6-1 RECYCLING PROBLEM, p. C-6

Reconciling a bank statement; journalizing a bank service charge, a dishonored check, and petty cash transactions

1., 3.

JOURNAL PAGE 12

DATE	ACCOUNT TITLE	DOC. NO.	POST. REF.	GENERAL DEBIT	GENERAL CREDIT	SALES CREDIT	CASH DEBIT	CASH CREDIT	
1									1
2									2
3									3
4									4
5									5
6									6
7									7
8									8
9									9
10									10
11									11
12									12

2.

RECONCILIATION OF BANK STATEMENT

_____ (Date)

Balance On Check Stub No. ___ .... $ _____
DEDUCT BANK CHARGES:

Description	Amount
	$

Total bank charges ▶

Balance On Bank Statement .... $ _____
ADD OUTSTANDING DEPOSITS:

Date	Amount
	$

Total outstanding deposits ▶

SUBTOTAL .... $ _____
DEDUCT OUTSTANDING CHECKS:

Ck. No.	Amount	Ck. No.	Amount

Total outstanding checks ▶

Adjusted Check Stub Balance .... $ _____

Adjusted Bank Balance .... $ _____

Extra forms

JOURNAL

PAGE

	DATE	ACCOUNT TITLE	DOC. NO.	POST. REF.	GENERAL DEBIT (1)	GENERAL CREDIT (2)	SALES CREDIT (3)	CASH DEBIT (4)	CASH CREDIT (5)	
1										1
2										2
3										3
4										4
5										5
6										6
7										7
8										8
9										9
10										10
11										11
12										12

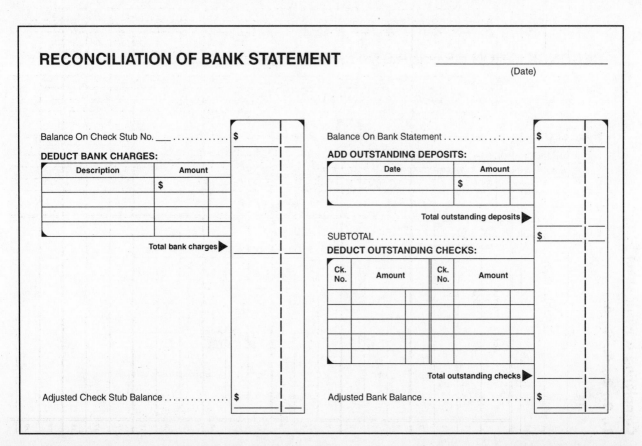

RECONCILIATION OF BANK STATEMENT

_____ (Date)

Balance On Check Stub No. ____ .... $ _____

DEDUCT BANK CHARGES:

Description	Amount
	$

Total bank charges ▶

Balance On Bank Statement .... $ _____

ADD OUTSTANDING DEPOSITS:

Date	Amount
	$

Total outstanding deposits ▶

SUBTOTAL .... $ _____

DEDUCT OUTSTANDING CHECKS:

Ck. No.	Amount	Ck. No.	Amount

Total outstanding checks ▶

Adjusted Check Stub Balance .... $ _____

Adjusted Bank Balance .... $ _____

7-1 RECYCLING PROBLEM, p. C-7

Completing a work sheet
1., 2., 3., 4., 5., 6.

ACCOUNT TITLE	TRIAL BALANCE		ADJUSTMENTS		INCOME STATEMENT		BALANCE SHEET	
	DEBIT	CREDIT	DEBIT	CREDIT	DEBIT	CREDIT	DEBIT	CREDIT
	1	2	3	4	5	6	7	8

Extra form

ACCOUNT TITLE	TRIAL BALANCE		ADJUSTMENTS		INCOME STATEMENT		BALANCE SHEET	
	DEBIT	CREDIT	DEBIT	CREDIT	DEBIT	CREDIT	DEBIT	CREDIT
	1	2	3	4	5	6	7	8
1								
2								
3								
4								
5								
6								
7								
8								
9								
10								
11								
12								
13								
14								
15								
16								
17								
18								
19								
20								
21								
22								
23								

8-1 RECYCLING PROBLEM, p. C-8

Preparing financial statements

1., 2.

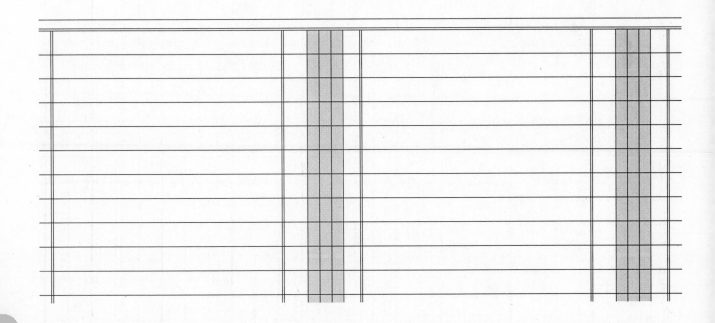

3.

Extra forms

			% OF SALES

9-1 **RECYCLING PROBLEM, p. C-9**

Journalizing adjusting and closing entries

1., 2.

JOURNAL

PAGE 16

	DATE	ACCOUNT TITLE	DOC. NO.	POST. REF.	GENERAL		SALES CREDIT	CASH	
					DEBIT	CREDIT		DEBIT	CREDIT
1									
2									
3									
4									
5									
6									
7									
8									
9									
10									
11									
12									
13									
14									
15									
16									
17									
18									
19									
20									
21									
22									
23									

Extra form

JOURNAL

					GENERAL		SALES	CASH		PAGE 5
					1	2	3	4	5	

DATE	ACCOUNT TITLE	DOC. NO.	POST. REF.	GENERAL DEBIT	GENERAL CREDIT	SALES CREDIT	CASH DEBIT	CASH CREDIT

Extra form

		5	6	7	8	9	10	11	
		SALES CREDIT	SALES TAX PAYABLE CREDIT	ACCOUNTS PAYABLE DEBIT	CREDIT	PURCHASES DEBIT	CASH DEBIT	CREDIT	
1									1
2									2
3									3
4									4
5									5
6									6
7									7
8									8
9									9
10									10
11									11
12									12
13									13
14									14
15									15
16									16
17									17
18									18
19									19
20									20
21									21
22									22
23									23
24									24
25									25
26									26
27									27
28									28
29									29
30									30
31									31
32									32
33									33

10-1 RECYCLING PROBLEM, p. C-10

Journalizing purchases, cash payments, and other transactions

PAGE 20

JOURNAL

	DATE	ACCOUNT TITLE	DOC. NO.	POST. REF.	GENERAL DEBIT	GENERAL CREDIT	ACCOUNTS RECEIVABLE DEBIT	ACCOUNTS RECEIVABLE CREDIT	
1									1
2									2
3									3
4									4
5									5
6									6
7									7
8									8
9									9
10									10
11									11
12									12
13									13
14									14
15									15
16									16
17									17
18									18
19									19
20									20
21									21
22									22
23									23
24									24
25									25
26									26
27									27
28									28
29									29
30									30
31									31
32									32
33									33

10-1 RECYCLING PROBLEM (concluded)

PAGE 20

	SALES CREDIT	SALES TAX PAYABLE CREDIT	ACCOUNTS PAYABLE		PURCHASES DEBIT	CASH		
	5	6	7 DEBIT	8 CREDIT	9	10 DEBIT	11 CREDIT	
1								1
2								2
3								3
4								4
5								5
6								6
7								7
8								8
9								9
10								10
11								11
12								12
13								13
14								14
15								15
16								16
17								17
18								18
19								19
20								20
21								21
22								22
23								23
24								24
25								25
26								26
27								27
28								28
29								29
30								30
31								31
32								32
33								33

Extra form

JOURNAL

	DATE	ACCOUNT TITLE	DOC. NO.	POST. REF.	GENERAL		ACCOUNTS RECEIVABLE		
					1 DEBIT	**2** CREDIT	**3** DEBIT	**4** CREDIT	
1									1
2									2
3									3
4									4
5									5
6									6
7									7
8									8
9									9
10									10
11									11
12									12
13									13
14									14
15									15
16									16
17									17
18									18
19									19
20									20
21									21
22									22
23									23
24									24
25									25
26									26
27									27
28									28
29									29
30									30
31									31
32									32
33									33

Extra forms

	5	6	7	8	9	10	11	
	SALES CREDIT	SALES TAX PAYABLE CREDIT	ACCOUNTS PAYABLE		PURCHASES DEBIT	CASH		
			DEBIT	CREDIT		DEBIT	CREDIT	
1								1
2								2
3								3
4								4
5								5
6								6
7								7
8								8
9								9
10								10
11								11
12								12
13								13
14								14
15								15
16								16
17								17
18								18

Col. No.	Column Title	Debit Totals	Credit Totals
1	General Debit	_____	
2	General Credit		_____
3	Accounts Receivable Debit	_____	
4	Accounts Receivable Credit		_____
5	Sales Credit		_____
6	Sales Tax Payable Credit		_____
7	Accounts Payable Debit	_____	
8	Accounts Payable Credit		_____
9	Purchases Debit	_____	
10	Cash Debit	_____	
11	Cash Credit		_____
	Totals	_____	_____

11-1 RECYCLING PROBLEM, p. C-11

Journalizing sales and cash receipts transactions; proving and ruling a journal

1.

PAGE 17   JOURNAL

	DATE	ACCOUNT TITLE	DOC. NO.	POST. REF.	GENERAL DEBIT	GENERAL CREDIT	ACCOUNTS RECEIVABLE DEBIT	ACCOUNTS RECEIVABLE CREDIT	
31									31
32	23						8 9 2 32	9 2 4 04	32

2., 3., 4., 5.

PAGE 18   JOURNAL

	DATE	ACCOUNT TITLE	DOC. NO.	POST. REF.	GENERAL DEBIT	GENERAL CREDIT	ACCOUNTS RECEIVABLE DEBIT	ACCOUNTS RECEIVABLE CREDIT	
1									1
2									2
3									3
4									4
5									5
6									6
7									7
8									8

1.

Col. No.	Column Title	Debit Totals	Credit Totals
1	General Debit	_____	
2	General Credit		_____
3	Accounts Receivable Debit	_____	
4	Accounts Receivable Credit		_____
5	Sales Credit		_____
6	Sales Tax Payable Credit		_____
7	Accounts Payable Debit . . .	_____	
8	Accounts Payable Credit . .		_____
9	Purchases Debit	_____	
10	Cash Debit	_____	
11	Cash Credit		_____
	Totals	_____	_____

2.

Col. No.	Column Title	Debit Totals	Credit Totals
1	General Debit	_____	
2	General Credit		_____
3	Accounts Receivable Debit	_____	
4	Accounts Receivable Credit		_____
5	Sales Credit		_____
6	Sales Tax Payable Credit		_____
7	Accounts Payable Debit . . .		_____
8	Accounts Payable Credit . .		_____
9	Purchases Debit	_____	
10	Cash Debit	_____	
11	Cash Credit		_____
	Totals	_____	_____

11-1 RECYCLING PROBLEM (concluded)

1.

PAGE 17

	SALES CREDIT	SALES TAX PAYABLE CREDIT	ACCOUNTS PAYABLE DEBIT	ACCOUNTS PAYABLE CREDIT	PURCHASES DEBIT	CASH DEBIT	CASH CREDIT	
	5	6	7	8	9	10	11	
31								31
32	16 7 8 3 00	1 0 0 6 98				17 8 2 1 70		32

2., 3., 4., 5.

PAGE 18

	SALES CREDIT	SALES TAX PAYABLE CREDIT	ACCOUNTS PAYABLE DEBIT	ACCOUNTS PAYABLE CREDIT	PURCHASES DEBIT	CASH DEBIT	CASH CREDIT	
	5	6	7	8	9	10	11	
1								1
2								2
3								3
4								4
5								5
6								6
7								7
8								8

4.

Col. No.	Column Title	Debit Totals	Credit Totals
1	General Debit	_____	
2	General Credit		_____
3	Accounts Receivable Debit	_____	
4	Accounts Receivable Credit		_____
5	Sales Credit		_____
6	Sales Tax Payable Credit		_____
7	Accounts Payable Debit . . .	_____	
8	Accounts Payable Credit . .		_____
9	Purchases Debit	_____	
10	Cash Debit	_____	
11	Cash Credit		_____
	Totals	_____	_____

Extra forms

JOURNAL

	DATE	ACCOUNT TITLE	DOC. NO.	POST. REF.	GENERAL		ACCOUNTS RECEIVABLE		
					1 DEBIT	2 CREDIT	3 DEBIT	4 CREDIT	
1									1
2									2
3									3
4									4
5									5
6									6
7									7
8									8
9									9
10									10
11									11
12									12
13									13
14									14
15									15
16									16
17									17
18									18

Col. No.	Column Title	Debit Totals	Credit Totals
1	General Debit	_____	
2	General Credit		_____
3	Accounts Receivable Debit	_____	
4	Accounts Receivable Credit		_____
5	Sales Credit		_____
6	Sales Tax Payable Credit		_____
7	Accounts Payable Debit	_____	
8	Accounts Payable Credit		_____
9	Purchases Debit	_____	
10	Cash Debit	_____	
11	Cash Credit		_____
	Totals	_____	_____

Extra form

12-1 RECYCLING PROBLEM, p. C-12

Posting to ledgers from a journal

1., 2.

JOURNAL

	DATE		ACCOUNT TITLE	DOC. NO.	POST. REF.	GENERAL DEBIT	GENERAL CREDIT	ACCOUNTS RECEIVABLE DEBIT	ACCOUNTS RECEIVABLE CREDIT	
1	20-- Aug.	1	Rent Expense	C219		1 3 0 0 00				1
2		2	Diamond T. Boots	P63						2
3		4	Gary Voyles	R29					3 6 7 50	3
4		5	✓	T5	✓					4
5		7	Utilities Expense	C220		2 2 1 34				5
6		9	Supplies—Office	M30		1 8 9 00				6
7			National Supply							7
8		10	Western Leather Co.	C221						8
9		12	✓	T12	✓					9
10		14	Joe Chapin	S50				3 8 2 20		10
11		15	Susan King	S51				1 8 3 75		11
12		15	Faye Garon, Drawing	C222		1 7 5 0 00				12
13		15	Lane Madison, Drawing	C223		1 7 5 0 00				13
14		18	Boot Town	P64						14
15		19	✓	T19	✓					15
16		22	Faye Garon, Drawing	M31		1 7 5 00				16
17			Purchases				1 7 5 00			17
18		24	Gary Voyles	S52				1 9 8 45		18
19		25	Joan Aberg	S53				1 3 9 65		19
20		26	✓	T26	✓					20
21		28	Joan Aberg	R30					2 4 9 90	21
22		28	Boot Town	C224						22
23		31	Supplies—Office	C225		5 8 80				23
24			Supplies—Store			8 0 50				24
25			Advertising Expense			8 9 60				25
26			Miscellaneous Expense			5 3 20				26
27		31	Western Leather Co.	P65						27
28		31	✓	T31	✓					28
29		31	Totals			5 6 6 7 44	1 7 5 00	9 0 4 05	6 1 7 40	29
30										30
31										31

12-1 RECYCLING PROBLEM (continued)

1., 2.

PAGE 9

	5 SALES CREDIT	6 SALES TAX PAYABLE CREDIT	7 ACCOUNTS PAYABLE DEBIT	8 ACCOUNTS PAYABLE CREDIT	9 PURCHASES DEBIT	10 CASH DEBIT	11 CASH CREDIT	
1							1 3 0 0 00	1
2			2 3 1 0 00	2 3 1 0 00				2
3						3 6 7 50		3
4	4 6 9 0 00	2 3 4 50				4 9 2 4 50		4
5							2 2 1 34	5
6								6
7				1 8 9 00				7
8			3 2 7 6 00				3 2 7 6 00	8
9	5 7 9 6 00	2 8 9 80				6 0 8 5 80		9
10	3 6 4 00	1 8 20						10
11	1 7 5 00	8 75						11
12							1 7 5 0 00	12
13							1 7 5 0 00	13
14				1 3 1 6 00	1 3 1 6 00			14
15	5 7 1 2 00	2 8 5 60				5 9 9 7 60		15
16								16
17								17
18	1 8 9 00	9 45						18
19	1 3 3 00	6 65						19
20	6 3 4 2 00	3 1 7 10				6 6 5 9 10		20
21						2 4 9 90		21
22			2 0 7 2 00				2 0 7 2 00	22
23							2 8 2 10	23
24								24
25								25
26								26
27				1 2 0 4 00	1 2 0 4 00			27
28	3 6 6 8 00	1 8 3 40				3 8 5 1 40		28
29	27 0 6 9 00	1 3 5 3 45	5 3 4 8 00	5 0 1 9 00	4 8 3 0 00	28 1 3 5 80	10 6 5 1 44	29
30								30
31								31

3.

12-1 RECYCLING PROBLEM (continued)

1., 2., 3.   **GENERAL LEDGER**

ACCOUNT Cash   ACCOUNT NO. 1110

DATE	ITEM	POST. REF.	DEBIT	CREDIT	BALANCE DEBIT	BALANCE CREDIT
20-- Aug. 1	Balance	✓			15 8 4 0 00	

ACCOUNT Accounts Receivable   ACCOUNT NO. 1130

DATE	ITEM	POST. REF.	DEBIT	CREDIT	BALANCE DEBIT	BALANCE CREDIT
20-- Aug. 1	Balance	✓			6 1 7 40	

ACCOUNT Supplies—Office   ACCOUNT NO. 1140

DATE	ITEM	POST. REF.	DEBIT	CREDIT	BALANCE DEBIT	BALANCE CREDIT
20-- Aug. 1	Balance	✓			2 1 9 6 00	

ACCOUNT Supplies—Store   ACCOUNT NO. 1150

DATE	ITEM	POST. REF.	DEBIT	CREDIT	BALANCE DEBIT	BALANCE CREDIT
20-- Aug. 1	Balance	✓			1 8 7 2 00	

ACCOUNT Accounts Payable   ACCOUNT NO. 2110

DATE	ITEM	POST. REF.	DEBIT	CREDIT	BALANCE DEBIT	BALANCE CREDIT
20-- Aug. 1	Balance	✓				5 3 4 8 00

ACCOUNT Sales Tax Payable   ACCOUNT NO. 2120

DATE	ITEM	POST. REF.	DEBIT	CREDIT	BALANCE DEBIT	BALANCE CREDIT
20-- Aug. 1	Balance	✓				1 1 2 5 00

1., 2., 3. GENERAL LEDGER

ACCOUNT Faye Garon, Drawing   ACCOUNT NO. 3120

DATE		ITEM	POST. REF.	DEBIT	CREDIT	BALANCE	
						DEBIT	CREDIT
20-- Aug.	1	Balance	✓			12 5 5 0 00	

ACCOUNT Lane Madison, Drawing   ACCOUNT NO. 3140

DATE		ITEM	POST. REF.	DEBIT	CREDIT	BALANCE	
						DEBIT	CREDIT
20-- Aug.	1	Balance	✓			12 2 5 0 00	

ACCOUNT Sales   ACCOUNT NO. 4110

DATE		ITEM	POST. REF.	DEBIT	CREDIT	BALANCE	
						DEBIT	CREDIT
20-- Aug.	1	Balance	✓				180 0 0 0 00

ACCOUNT Purchases   ACCOUNT NO. 5110

DATE		ITEM	POST. REF.	DEBIT	CREDIT	BALANCE	
						DEBIT	CREDIT
20-- Aug.	1	Balance	✓			105 6 0 0 00	

ACCOUNT Advertising Expense   ACCOUNT NO. 6110

DATE		ITEM	POST. REF.	DEBIT	CREDIT	BALANCE	
						DEBIT	CREDIT
20-- Aug.	1	Balance	✓			2 7 7 0 00	

ACCOUNT Miscellaneous Expense   ACCOUNT NO. 6140

DATE		ITEM	POST. REF.	DEBIT	CREDIT	BALANCE	
						DEBIT	CREDIT
20-- Aug.	1	Balance	✓			1 5 2 0 00	

12-1 RECYCLING PROBLEM (continued)

1., 2., 3.   **GENERAL LEDGER**

ACCOUNT Rent Expense   ACCOUNT NO. 6160

DATE		ITEM	POST. REF.	DEBIT	CREDIT	BALANCE	
						DEBIT	CREDIT
20-- Aug.	1	Balance	✓			9 1 0 0 00	

ACCOUNT Utilities Expense   ACCOUNT NO. 6190

DATE		ITEM	POST. REF.	DEBIT	CREDIT	BALANCE	
						DEBIT	CREDIT
20-- Aug.	1	Balance	✓			2 2 6 0 00	

1., 3.   **ACCOUNTS PAYABLE LEDGER**

VENDOR Boot Town   VENDOR NO. 210

DATE		ITEM	POST. REF.	DEBIT	CREDIT	CREDIT BALANCE
20-- Aug.	1	Balance	✓			2 0 7 2 00

VENDOR Diamond T. Boots   VENDOR NO. 220

DATE		ITEM	POST. REF.	DEBIT	CREDIT	CREDIT BALANCE

VENDOR National Supply   VENDOR NO. 230

DATE		ITEM	POST. REF.	DEBIT	CREDIT	CREDIT BALANCE

VENDOR Western Leather Co.   VENDOR NO. 240

DATE		ITEM	POST. REF.	DEBIT	CREDIT	CREDIT BALANCE
20-- Aug.	1	Balance	✓			3 2 7 6 00

1., 3.

ACCOUNTS RECEIVABLE LEDGER

CUSTOMER Joan Aberg   CUSTOMER NO. 110

DATE		ITEM	POST. REF.	DEBIT	CREDIT	DEBIT BALANCE
20-- Aug.	1	Balance	✓			2 4 9 90

CUSTOMER Joe Chapin   CUSTOMER NO. 120

DATE		ITEM	POST. REF.	DEBIT	CREDIT	DEBIT BALANCE

CUSTOMER Susan King   CUSTOMER NO. 130

DATE		ITEM	POST. REF.	DEBIT	CREDIT	DEBIT BALANCE

CUSTOMER Gary Voyles   CUSTOMER NO. 140

DATE		ITEM	POST. REF.	DEBIT	CREDIT	DEBIT BALANCE
20-- Aug.	1	Balance	✓			3 6 7 50

13-1 RECYCLING PROBLEM, p. C-13

Preparing semimonthly payroll

1., 3.

PAYROLL REGISTER

EMPL. NO.	EMPLOYEE'S NAME	MARI-TAL STATUS	NO. OF ALLOW-ANCES	EARNINGS			DEDUCTIONS						NET PAY	CHECK NO.
				REGULAR	OVERTIME	TOTAL	FEDERAL INCOME TAX	SOC. SEC. TAX	MEDICARE TAX	HEALTH INSURANCE	OTHER	TOTAL		
				1	2	3	4	5	6	7	8	9	10	
1														
2														
3														
4														
5														
6														
7														
8														
9														
10														
11														
12														
13														
14														
15														
16														
17														
18														
19														
20														
21														
22														

SEMIMONTHLY PERIOD ENDED

DATE OF PAYMENT

OTHER DEDUCTIONS: B—U.S. SAVINGS BONDS; UW—UNITED WAY

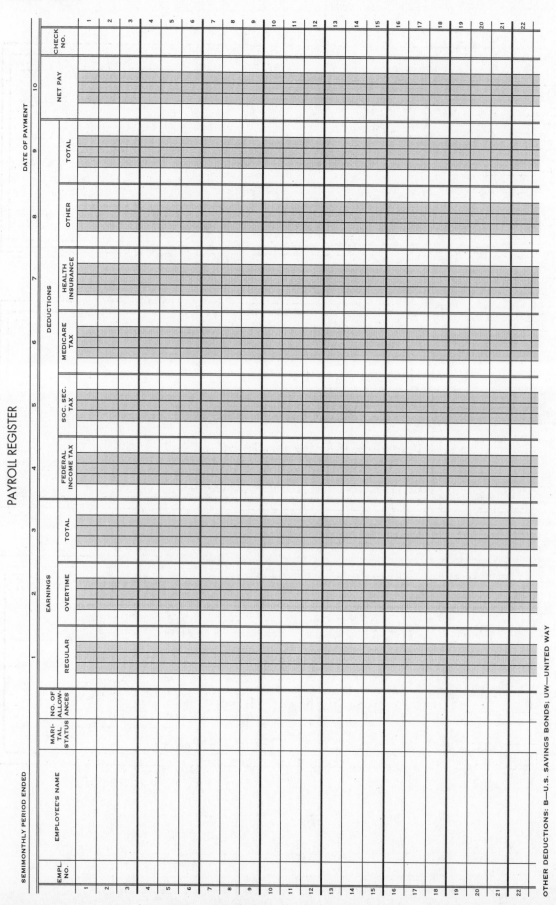

PAYROLL REGISTER

Name _____ Date _____ Class _____

2., 3.

NO. **630**

Date: _____ 20___ $_____

To: _____

For: _____

BAL. BRO'T FOR'D				
AMT. DEPOSITED				
TOTAL				
AMT. THIS CHECK				
BAL. CAR'D FOR'D				

GENERAL ACCOUNT   NO. **630**   66-877 / 530

McKINLEY COMPANY

_____ 20 _____

PAY TO THE
ORDER OF _____ $ _____

_____ DOLLARS

For Classroom Use Only

Peoples Bank and Trust
Charlotte, NC 28206-8444

⑆053008774⑆ 196‖2236‖42‖

CHECK NO. **286**

PERIOD ENDING		
EARNINGS	$	
REG.	$	
O.T.	$	
DEDUCTIONS	$	
INC. TAX	$	
SOC. SEC. TAX	$	
MED. TAX	$	
HEALTH INS.	$	
OTHER	$	
NET PAY	$	

PAYROLL ACCOUNT   66-877 / 530

_____ 20 _____   NO. **286**

PAY TO THE
ORDER OF _____ $ _____

_____ DOLLARS

For Classroom Use Only

McKINLEY COMPANY

Peoples Bank and Trust
Charlotte, NC 28206-8444

⑆053008774⑆ 196‖2236‖44‖

CHECK NO. **289**

PERIOD ENDING		
EARNINGS	$	
REG.	$	
O.T.	$	
DEDUCTIONS	$	
INC. TAX	$	
SOC. SEC. TAX	$	
MED. TAX	$	
HEALTH INS.	$	
OTHER	$	
NET PAY	$	

PAYROLL ACCOUNT   66-877 / 530

_____ 20 _____   NO. **289**

PAY TO THE
ORDER OF _____ $ _____

_____ DOLLARS

For Classroom Use Only

McKINLEY COMPANY

Peoples Bank and Trust
Charlotte, NC 28206-8444

⑆053008774⑆ 196‖2236‖44‖

Extra forms

NO. **630**

Date: _____ 20____ $_____

To: _____

_____

For: _____

_____

BAL. BRO'T FOR'D			
AMT. DEPOSITED			
TOTAL			
AMT. THIS CHECK			
BAL. CAR'D FOR'D			

GENERAL ACCOUNT NO. **630** 66-877 / 530

McKINLEY COMPANY

_____ 20 _____

PAY TO THE ORDER OF _____ $ _____

_____ DOLLARS

For Classroom Use Only

Peoples Bank and Trust

Charlotte, NC 28206-8444

⑆05300877⑆: 196⑈2236⑈42⑈

CHECK NO. **286**

PERIOD ENDING		
EARNINGS	$	
REG.	$	
O.T.	$	
DEDUCTIONS	$	
INC. TAX	$	
SOC. SEC. TAX	$	
MED. TAX	$	
HEALTH INS.	$	
OTHER	$	
NET PAY	$	

PAYROLL ACCOUNT 66-877 / 530

_____ 20 _____

NO. **286**

PAY TO THE ORDER OF _____ $ _____

_____ DOLLARS

For Classroom Use Only

McKINLEY COMPANY

Peoples Bank and Trust

Charlotte, NC 28206-8444

⑆05300877⑆: 196⑈2236⑈44⑈

CHECK NO. **289**

PERIOD ENDING		
EARNINGS	$	
REG.	$	
O.T.	$	
DEDUCTIONS	$	
INC. TAX	$	
SOC. SEC. TAX	$	
MED. TAX	$	
HEALTH INS.	$	
OTHER	$	
NET PAY	$	

PAYROLL ACCOUNT 66-877 / 530

_____ 20 _____

NO. **289**

PAY TO THE ORDER OF _____ $ _____

_____ DOLLARS

For Classroom Use Only

McKINLEY COMPANY

Peoples Bank and Trust

Charlotte, NC 28206-8444

⑆05300877⑆: 196⑈2236⑈44⑈

Name _____ Date _____ Class _____

14-1 RECYCLING PROBLEM, p. C-14

Journalizing payroll taxes

1., 2.

PAGE 3   JOURNAL   PAGE 3

	DATE	ACCOUNT TITLE	DOC. NO.	POST. REF.	GENERAL DEBIT 1	GENERAL CREDIT 2		CASH DEBIT 10	CASH CREDIT 11	
1										1
2										2
3										3
4										4
5										5
6										6
7										7
8										8
9										9
10										10
11										11
12										12
13										13
14										14
15										15
16										16
17										17
18										18
19										19
20										20
21										21
22										22
23										23
24										24
25										25
26										26
27										27
28										28
29										29
30										30
31										31

RECYCLING PROBLEM (concluded)

2., 3., 4.

PAGE 4   JOURNAL   PAGE 4

	DATE	ACCOUNT TITLE	DOC. NO.	POST. REF.	GENERAL DEBIT	GENERAL CREDIT	CASH DEBIT	CASH CREDIT	
1									1
2									2
3									3
4									4
5									5
6									6
7									7
8									8
9									9
10									10
11									11
12									12
13									13
14									14
15									15
16									16
17									17
18									18
19									19
20									20
21									21
22									22
23									23
24									24
25									25
26									26
27									27
28									28
29									29
30									30
31									31

15-1 RECYCLING PROBLEM, p. C-15

Preparing an 8-column work sheet for a merchandising business

1., 2.

Jolson Music
Work Sheet
For Year Ended December 31, 20-- --

ACCOUNT TITLE	TRIAL BALANCE DEBIT	TRIAL BALANCE CREDIT	ADJUSTMENTS DEBIT	ADJUSTMENTS CREDIT	INCOME STATEMENT DEBIT	INCOME STATEMENT CREDIT	BALANCE SHEET DEBIT	BALANCE SHEET CREDIT
1 Cash	24 640 00							
2 Petty Cash	5 00 00							
3 Accounts Receivable	11 1 15 00							
4 Merchandise Inventory	267 9 80 00							
5 Supplies—Office	6 1 0 0 00							
6 Supplies—Store	6 5 0 0 00							
7 Prepaid Insurance	5 1 6 0 00							
8 Accounts Payable		11 6 6 5 00						
9 Sales Tax Payable		1 1 4 0 00						
10 Kristin Jolson, Capital		128 8 4 0 00						
11 Kristin Jolson, Drawing	20 5 0 0 00							
12 Albert Jolson, Capital		127 4 3 0 00						
13 Albert Jolson, Drawing	20 3 5 0 00							
14 Income Summary								
15 Sales		227 4 5 0 00						
16 Purchases	102 3 0 0 00							
17 Advertising Expense	5 6 8 0 00							
18 Credit Card Fee Expense	2 3 1 5 00							
19 Insurance Expense								
20 Miscellaneous Expense	2 8 3 0 00							
21 Rent Expense	17 2 8 0 00							
22 Supplies Expense—Office								
23 Supplies Expense—Store								
24 Utilities Expense	3 2 7 5 00							
25	496 5 2 5 00	496 5 2 5 00						
26								
27								

Extra form

ACCOUNT TITLE		TRIAL BALANCE		ADJUSTMENTS		INCOME STATEMENT		BALANCE SHEET	
		DEBIT	CREDIT	DEBIT	CREDIT	DEBIT	CREDIT	DEBIT	CREDIT
		1	2	3	4	5	6	7	8
1									
2									
3									
4									
5									
6									
7									
8									
9									
10									
11									
12									
13									
14									
15									
16									
17									
18									
19									
20									
21									
22									
23									
24									
25									
26									
27									

16-1 RECYCLING PROBLEM, p. C-16

Preparing financial statements

1.

				% OF SALES

2.

3.

16-1 RECYCLING PROBLEM (concluded)

4.

Extra form

17-1 RECYCLING PROBLEM, p. C-17

Journalizing adjusting and closing entries

1., 2.

PAGE 25   JOURNAL

	DATE	ACCOUNT TITLE	DOC. NO.	POST. REF.	GENERAL DEBIT	GENERAL CREDIT	ACCOUNTS RECEIVABLE DEBIT	ACCOUNTS RECEIVABLE CREDIT	
1									1
2									2
3									3
4									4
5									5
6									6
7									7
8									8
9									9
10									10
11									11
12									12
13									13
14									14
15									15
16									16
17									17
18									18
19									19
20									20
21									21
22									22
23									23
24									24
25									25
26									26
27									27
28									28
29									29
30									30
31									31

Extra form

JOURNAL

	DATE	ACCOUNT TITLE	DOC. NO.	POST. REF.	GENERAL		ACCOUNTS RECEIVABLE		
					DEBIT	CREDIT	DEBIT	CREDIT	
1									1
2									2
3									3
4									4
5									5
6									6
7									7
8									8
9									9
10									10
11									11
12									12
13									13
14									14
15									15
16									16
17									17
18									18
19									19
20									20
21									21
22									22
23									23
24									24
25									25
26									26
27									27
28									28
29									29
30									30
31									31
32									32
33									33

18-1 RECYCLING PROBLEM, p. C-18

Journalizing and posting purchases and cash payment transactions

1., 2.

PURCHASES JOURNAL   PAGE 7

	DATE		ACCOUNT CREDITED	PURCH. NO.	POST. REF.	PURCHASES DR. ACCTS. PAY. CR.	
1							1
2							2
3							3
4							4
5							5
6							6
7							7
8							8
9							9
10							10

1.

GENERAL JOURNAL   PAGE 7

	DATE		ACCOUNT TITLE	DOC. NO.	POST. REF.	DEBIT	CREDIT	
1								1
2								2
3								3
4								4
5								5
6								6
7								7
8								8
9								9
10								10
11								11
12								12
13								13

1., 3.

CASH PAYMENTS JOURNAL

PAGE 11

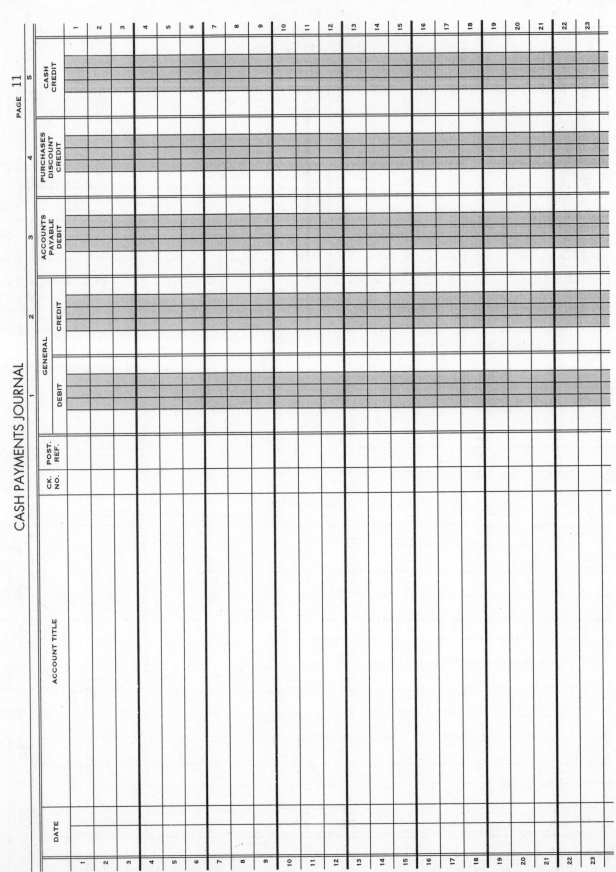

	DATE	ACCOUNT TITLE	CK. NO.	POST. REF.	GENERAL DEBIT	GENERAL CREDIT	ACCOUNTS PAYABLE DEBIT	PURCHASES DISCOUNT CREDIT	CASH CREDIT	
					1	2	3	4	5	
1										1
2										2
3										3
4										4
5										5
6										6
7										7
8										8
9										9
10										10
11										11
12										12
13										13
14										14
15										15
16										16
17										17
18										18
19										19
20										20
21										21
22										22
23										23

18-1 **RECYCLING PROBLEM (continued)**

4.

1., 2., 3., 4.   **GENERAL LEDGER**

ACCOUNT Cash   ACCOUNT NO. 1105

DATE		ITEM	POST. REF.	DEBIT	CREDIT	BALANCE DEBIT	BALANCE CREDIT
20-- July	1	Balance	✓			15 4 8 3 00	

ACCOUNT Petty Cash   ACCOUNT NO. 1110

DATE		ITEM	POST. REF.	DEBIT	CREDIT	BALANCE DEBIT	BALANCE CREDIT
20-- July	1	Balance	✓			2 5 0 00	

ACCOUNT Supplies   ACCOUNT NO. 1140

DATE		ITEM	POST. REF.	DEBIT	CREDIT	BALANCE DEBIT	BALANCE CREDIT
20-- July	1	Balance	✓			3 5 1 5 00	

ACCOUNT Accounts Payable   ACCOUNT NO. 2115

DATE		ITEM	POST. REF.	DEBIT	CREDIT	BALANCE DEBIT	BALANCE CREDIT
20-- July	1	Balance	✓				7 4 7 2 00

ACCOUNT Purchases   ACCOUNT NO. 5105

DATE		ITEM	POST. REF.	DEBIT	CREDIT	BALANCE DEBIT	BALANCE CREDIT
20-- July	1	Balance	✓			84 1 8 6 00	

18-1 RECYCLING PROBLEM (continued)

1., 2., 3., 4.   **GENERAL LEDGER**

ACCOUNT Purchases Discount   ACCOUNT NO. 5110

DATE		ITEM	POST. REF.	DEBIT	CREDIT	BALANCE	
						DEBIT	CREDIT
July 1		Balance	✓				1 8 4 8 00

ACCOUNT Purchases Returns and Allowances   ACCOUNT NO. 5115

DATE		ITEM	POST. REF.	DEBIT	CREDIT	BALANCE	
						DEBIT	CREDIT
July 1		Balance	✓				2 8 1 0 00

ACCOUNT Advertising Expense   ACCOUNT NO. 6105

DATE		ITEM	POST. REF.	DEBIT	CREDIT	BALANCE	
						DEBIT	CREDIT
July 1		Balance	✓			3 5 1 5 80	

ACCOUNT Cash Short and Over   ACCOUNT NO. 6110

DATE		ITEM	POST. REF.	DEBIT	CREDIT	BALANCE	
						DEBIT	CREDIT
July 1		Balance	✓			1 58	

ACCOUNT Miscellaneous Expense   ACCOUNT NO. 6135

DATE		ITEM	POST. REF.	DEBIT	CREDIT	BALANCE	
						DEBIT	CREDIT
July 1		Balance	✓			1 3 5 2 50	

ACCOUNT Rent Expense   ACCOUNT NO. 6145

DATE		ITEM	POST. REF.	DEBIT	CREDIT	BALANCE	
						DEBIT	CREDIT
July 1		Balance	✓			3 6 0 0 00	

RECYCLING PROBLEM (concluded)

1., 4.   **ACCOUNTS PAYABLE LEDGER**

VENDOR Carson Company   VENDOR NO. 210

DATE		ITEM	POST. REF.	DEBIT	CREDIT	CREDIT BALANCE
20-- July	1	Balance	✓			1 3 6 4 00

VENDOR Delmar, Inc.   VENDOR NO. 220

DATE		ITEM	POST. REF.	DEBIT	CREDIT	CREDIT BALANCE

VENDOR Garrison Supply   VENDOR NO. 230

DATE		ITEM	POST. REF.	DEBIT	CREDIT	CREDIT BALANCE
20-- July	1	Balance	✓			2 0 6 8 00

VENDOR Macon Wire Company   VENDOR NO. 240

DATE		ITEM	POST. REF.	DEBIT	CREDIT	CREDIT BALANCE
20-- July	1	Balance	✓			1 5 6 0 00

VENDOR Sanders Company   VENDOR NO. 250

DATE		ITEM	POST. REF.	DEBIT	CREDIT	CREDIT BALANCE
20-- July	1	Balance	✓			2 4 8 0 00

19-1 RECYCLING PROBLEM, p. C-19

Journalizing and posting sales transactions

1., 2., 3.

SALES JOURNAL

	DATE		ACCOUNT DEBITED	SALE NO.	POST. REF.	1 ACCOUNTS RECEIVABLE DEBIT	2 SALES CREDIT	3 SALES TAX PAYABLE CREDIT	
1									1
2									2
3									3
4									4
5									5
6									6
7									7

1.

GENERAL JOURNAL

	DATE		ACCOUNT TITLE	DOC. NO.	POST. REF.	DEBIT	CREDIT	
1								1
2								2
3								3
4								4
5								5
6								6
7								7
8								8
9								9
10								10
11								11
12								12
13								13
14								14
15								15
16								16
17								17
18								18

1., 4., 5.

CASH RECEIPTS JOURNAL

PAGE 3

| | | | | | GENERAL | | ACCOUNTS RECEIVABLE | SALES | SALES TAX PAYABLE | | SALES DISCOUNT | CASH |
	DATE	ACCOUNT TITLE	DOC. NO.	POST. REF.	DEBIT	CREDIT	CREDIT	CREDIT	DEBIT	CREDIT	DEBIT	DEBIT
					1	2	3	4	5	6	7	8
1												
2												
3												
4												
5												
6												
7												
8												
9												
10												
11												
12												
13												
14												
15												
16												
17												
18												
19												
20												
21												
22												
23												

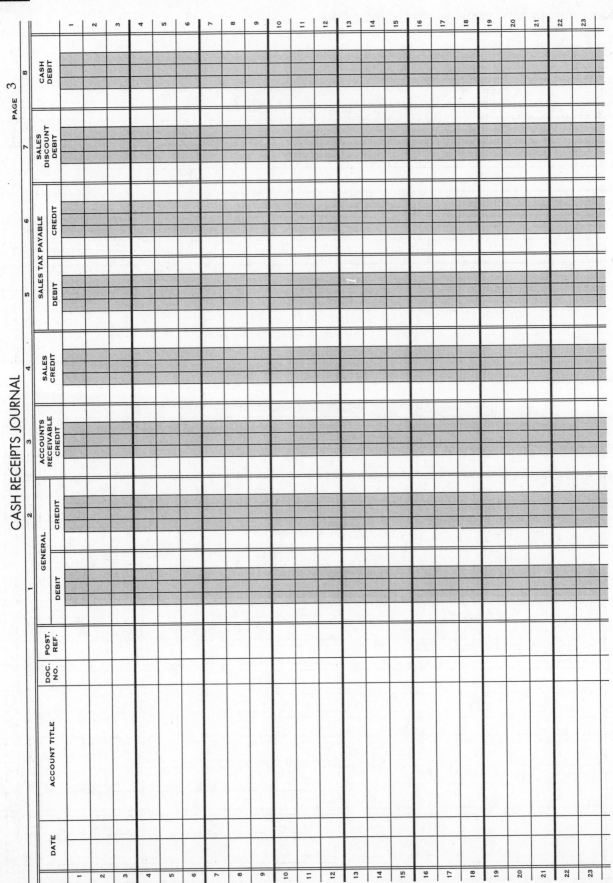

CENTURY 21 ACCOUNTING, 7TH EDITION

19-1 **RECYCLING PROBLEM** (continued)

6.

RECYCLING PROBLEM (continued)

1., 3., 5., 6.   **GENERAL LEDGER**

ACCOUNT Cash   ACCOUNT NO. 1105

DATE	ITEM	POST. REF.	DEBIT	CREDIT	BALANCE DEBIT	BALANCE CREDIT
20-- Mar. 1	Balance	✓			12 5 4 8 00	

ACCOUNT Accounts Receivable   ACCOUNT NO. 1125

DATE	ITEM	POST. REF.	DEBIT	CREDIT	BALANCE DEBIT	BALANCE CREDIT
20-- Mar. 1	Balance	✓			4 5 3 0 64	

ACCOUNT Time Drafts Receivable   ACCOUNT NO. 1130

DATE	ITEM	POST. REF.	DEBIT	CREDIT	BALANCE DEBIT	BALANCE CREDIT
20-- Mar. 1	Balance	✓			16 5 0 0 00	

ACCOUNT Sales Tax Payable   ACCOUNT NO. 2140

DATE	ITEM	POST. REF.	DEBIT	CREDIT	BALANCE DEBIT	BALANCE CREDIT
20-- Mar. 1	Balance	✓				7 4 2 50

19-1 **RECYCLING PROBLEM (continued)**

1., 3., 5., 6. **GENERAL LEDGER**

ACCOUNT Sales   ACCOUNT NO. 4105

DATE		ITEM	POST. REF.	DEBIT	CREDIT	BALANCE DEBIT	BALANCE CREDIT
20-- Mar.	1	Balance	✓				42 4 8 1 80

ACCOUNT Sales Discount   ACCOUNT NO. 4110

DATE		ITEM	POST. REF.	DEBIT	CREDIT	BALANCE DEBIT	BALANCE CREDIT
20-- Mar.	1	Balance	✓			3 9 80	

ACCOUNT Sales Returns and Allowances   ACCOUNT NO. 4115

DATE		ITEM	POST. REF.	DEBIT	CREDIT	BALANCE DEBIT	BALANCE CREDIT
20-- Mar.	1	Balance	✓			2 5 8 00	

1., 6. **ACCOUNTS RECEIVABLE LEDGER**

CUSTOMER Sandy Acker   CUSTOMER NO. 110

DATE	ITEM	POST. REF.	DEBIT	CREDIT	DEBIT BALANCE

CUSTOMER Clark, Inc.   CUSTOMER NO. 120

DATE		ITEM	POST. REF.	DEBIT	CREDIT	DEBIT BALANCE
20-- Mar.	1	Balance	✓			3 5 2 00

RECYCLING PROBLEM (concluded)

1., 6.

ACCOUNTS RECEIVABLE LEDGER

CUSTOMER Clayton Company   CUSTOMER NO. 130

DATE		ITEM	POST. REF.	DEBIT	CREDIT	DEBIT BALANCE
Mar. 20--	1	Balance	✓			4 5 3 60

CUSTOMER John Maxwell   CUSTOMER NO. 140

DATE		ITEM	POST. REF.	DEBIT	CREDIT	DEBIT BALANCE
Mar. 20--	1	Balance	✓			6 4 80

CUSTOMER Emily Parsons   CUSTOMER NO. 150

DATE		ITEM	POST. REF.	DEBIT	CREDIT	DEBIT BALANCE
Mar. 20--	1	Balance	✓			2 6 3 24

CUSTOMER Reston Company   CUSTOMER NO. 160

DATE		ITEM	POST. REF.	DEBIT	CREDIT	DEBIT BALANCE
Mar. 20--	1	Balance	✓			5 6 7 00

CUSTOMER Sawyer Supply   CUSTOMER NO. 170

DATE		ITEM	POST. REF.	DEBIT	CREDIT	DEBIT BALANCE

CUSTOMER Valley High School   CUSTOMER NO. 180

DATE		ITEM	POST. REF.	DEBIT	CREDIT	DEBIT BALANCE
Mar. 20--	1	Balance	✓			1 3 4 5 00

CUSTOMER Walsh Associates   CUSTOMER NO. 190

DATE		ITEM	POST. REF.	DEBIT	CREDIT	DEBIT BALANCE
Mar. 20--	1	Balance	✓			1 4 8 5 00

20-1 RECYCLING PROBLEM, p. C-20

Recording entries for uncollectible accounts

1.

GENERAL JOURNAL   PAGE 10

	DATE	ACCOUNT TITLE	DOC. NO.	POST. REF.	DEBIT	CREDIT	
1							1
2							2
3							3
4							4

2.

GENERAL JOURNAL   PAGE 11

	DATE	ACCOUNT TITLE	DOC. NO.	POST. REF.	DEBIT	CREDIT	
1							1
2							2
3							3
4							4
5							5
6							6

3.

GENERAL JOURNAL   PAGE 12

	DATE	ACCOUNT TITLE	DOC. NO.	POST. REF.	DEBIT	CREDIT	
1							1
2							2
3							3
4							4
5							5
6							6

4.

GENERAL JOURNAL   PAGE 13

	DATE	ACCOUNT TITLE	DOC. NO.	POST. REF.	DEBIT	CREDIT	
1							1
2							2
3							3

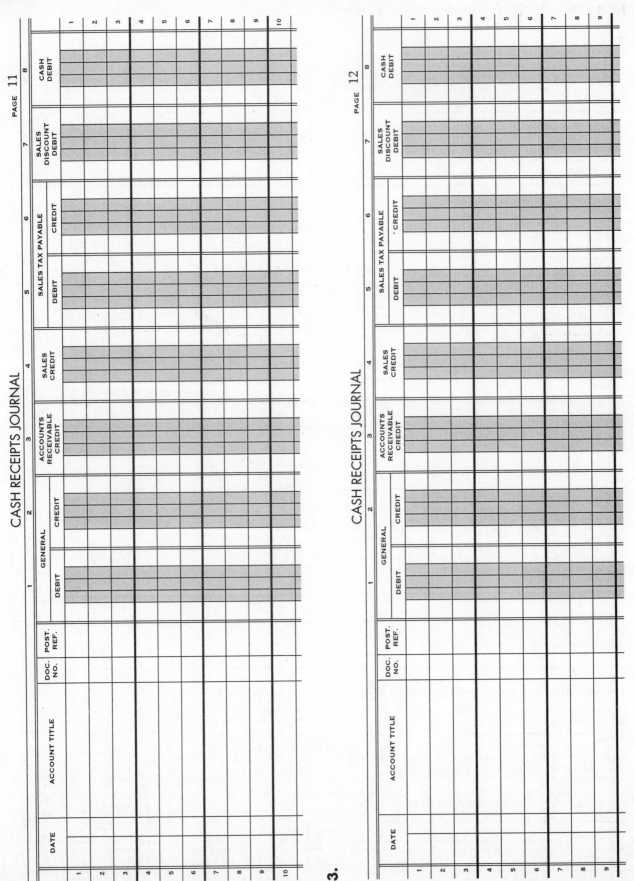

2.

CASH RECEIPTS JOURNAL

PAGE 11

DATE	ACCOUNT TITLE	DOC. NO.	POST. REF.	GENERAL DEBIT	GENERAL CREDIT	ACCOUNTS RECEIVABLE CREDIT	SALES CREDIT	SALES TAX PAYABLE DEBIT	SALES TAX PAYABLE CREDIT	SALES DISCOUNT DEBIT	CASH DEBIT

3.

CASH RECEIPTS JOURNAL

PAGE 12

DATE	ACCOUNT TITLE	DOC. NO.	POST. REF.	GENERAL DEBIT	GENERAL CREDIT	ACCOUNTS RECEIVABLE CREDIT	SALES CREDIT	SALES TAX PAYABLE DEBIT	SALES TAX PAYABLE CREDIT	SALES DISCOUNT DEBIT	CASH DEBIT

20-1 RECYCLING PROBLEM (continued)

1., 2., 3., 4.

GENERAL LEDGER

ACCOUNT Cash   ACCOUNT NO. 1105

DATE	ITEM	POST. REF.	DEBIT	CREDIT	BALANCE DEBIT	BALANCE CREDIT
20-- Oct. 1	Balance	✓			4 9 7 8 00	

ACCOUNT Accounts Receivable   ACCOUNT NO. 1125

DATE	ITEM	POST. REF.	DEBIT	CREDIT	BALANCE DEBIT	BALANCE CREDIT
20-- Oct. 1	Balance	✓			62 4 8 6 25	

ACCOUNT Allowance for Uncollectible Accounts   ACCOUNT NO. 1130

DATE	ITEM	POST. REF.	DEBIT	CREDIT	BALANCE DEBIT	BALANCE CREDIT
20-- Oct. 1	Balance	✓				2 4 1 8 19

ACCOUNT Uncollectible Accounts Expense   ACCOUNT NO. 6165

DATE	ITEM	POST. REF.	DEBIT	CREDIT	BALANCE DEBIT	BALANCE CREDIT

1., 2., 3.

ACCOUNTS RECEIVABLE LEDGER

CUSTOMER Agnew Company   CUSTOMER NO. 110

DATE		ITEM	POST. REF.	DEBIT	CREDIT	DEBIT BALANCE
20-- June	7		S6	8 0 4 24		8 0 4 24

CUSTOMER Chittenden Corp.   CUSTOMER NO. 120

DATE		ITEM	POST. REF.	DEBIT	CREDIT	DEBIT BALANCE
20-- May	13		S5	2 8 4 75		2 8 4 75

CUSTOMER Dionne, Inc.   CUSTOMER NO. 130

DATE		ITEM	POST. REF.	DEBIT	CREDIT	DEBIT BALANCE
20-- Jan.	1	Balance	✓			4 6 8 30
Mar.	3	Written off	G3		4 6 8 30	—

CUSTOMER Foster Corp.   CUSTOMER NO. 140

DATE		ITEM	POST. REF.	DEBIT	CREDIT	DEBIT BALANCE
20-- June	21		S6	5 7 4 10		5 7 4 10

CUSTOMER Grant Company   CUSTOMER NO. 150

DATE		ITEM	POST. REF.	DEBIT	CREDIT	DEBIT BALANCE
20-- Jan.	1	Balance	✓			7 0 5 18

21-1 **RECYCLING PROBLEM, p. C-21**

Recording transactions for plant assets

1.

CASH PAYMENTS JOURNAL

PAGE 1

DATE	ACCOUNT TITLE	CK. NO.	POST. REF.	GENERAL DEBIT	GENERAL CREDIT	ACCOUNTS PAYABLE DEBIT	PURCHASES DISCOUNT CREDIT	CASH CREDIT

5.

CASH RECEIPTS JOURNAL

PAGE 2

DATE	ACCOUNT TITLE	DOC. NO.	POST. REF.	GENERAL DEBIT	GENERAL CREDIT	ACCOUNTS RECEIVABLE CREDIT	SALES CREDIT	SALES TAX PAYABLE DEBIT	SALES TAX PAYABLE CREDIT	SALES DISCOUNT DEBIT	CASH DEBIT

5.

GENERAL JOURNAL   PAGE 2

	DATE		ACCOUNT TITLE	DOC. NO.	POST. REF.	DEBIT	CREDIT	
1								1
2								2
3								3
4								4
5								5
6								6
7								7
8								8
9								9
10								10
11								11
12								12
13								13
14								14
15								15
16								16
17								17
18								18
19								19
20								20
21								21
22								22
23								23
24								24
25								25
26								26
27								27
28								28
29								29
30								30
31								31
32								32
33								33

21-1 RECYCLING PROBLEM (continued)

2., 4., 6.

PLANT ASSET RECORD No. _____   General Ledger Account No. _____

Description _____   General Ledger Account _____

Date
Bought _____   Serial
                             Number _____   Original Cost _____

Estimated   Estimated
Useful Life _____   Salvage   Depreciation
                             Value _____   Method _____

Disposed of: Discarded _____   Sold _____   Traded _____

Date _____   Disposal Amount _____

YEAR	ANNUAL DEPRECIATION EXPENSE	ACCUMULATED DEPRECIATION	ENDING BOOK VALUE

Continue record on back of card

3.

Plant asset: _____   Original cost: _____
Depreciation method: _____   Estimated salvage value: _____
                                               Estimated useful life: _____

Year	Beginning Book Value	Declining-Balance Rate	Annual Depreciation	Ending Book Value

2., 4., 6.

PLANT ASSET RECORD No. _____   General Ledger Account No. _____

Description _____   General Ledger Account _____

Date   Serial
Bought _____   Number _____   Original Cost _____

                         Estimated
Estimated   Salvage   Depreciation
Useful Life _____   Value _____   Method   _____

Disposed of: Discarded _____   Sold _____   Traded _____
Date _____   Disposal Amount _____

YEAR	ANNUAL DEPRECIATION EXPENSE	ACCUMULATED DEPRECIATION	ENDING BOOK VALUE

Continue record on back of card

3.

Plant asset: _____   Original cost: _____
Depreciation method: _____   Estimated salvage value: _____
                                              Estimated useful life: _____

Year	Beginning Book Value	Annual Balance Rate	Accumulated Depreciation	Ending Book Value

22-1 RECYCLING PROBLEM, p. C-22

Determining the cost of inventory using the fifo, lifo, and weighted-average inventory costing methods

1.

FIFO Method

Purchase Dates	Units Purchased	Unit Price	Total Cost	FIFO Units on Hand	FIFO Cost
January 1, beginning inventory					
January 3, purchases					
March 29, purchases					
August 15, purchases					
November 13, purchases					
Totals					

LIFO Method

Purchase Dates	Units Purchased	Unit Price	Total Cost	LIFO Units on Hand	LIFO Cost
January 1, beginning inventory					
January 3, purchases					
March 29, purchases					
August 15, purchases					
November 13, purchases					
Totals					

Weighted-Average Method

Purchases			Total Cost
Date	Units	Unit Price	
January 1, beginning inventory			
January 3, purchases			
March 29, purchases			
August 15, purchases			
November 13, purchases			
Totals			

	Fifo	Lifo	Weighted Average
Merchandise Available for Sale			
Ending Inventory			
Cost of Merchandise Sold			

Highest Cost of Merchandise Sold:

Extra forms

FIFO Method

Purchase Dates	Units Purchased	Unit Price	Total Cost	FIFO Units on Hand	FIFO Cost

LIFO Method

Purchase Dates	Units Purchased	Unit Price	Total Cost	LIFO Units on Hand	LIFO Cost

Weighted-Average Method

Purchases			Total Cost
Date	Units	Unit Price	

	Fifo	Lifo	Weighted Average
Merchandise Available for Sale			
Ending Inventory			
Cost of Merchandise Sold			

Highest Cost of Merchandise Sold:

23-1 RECYCLING PROBLEM, p. C-23

Journalizing notes payable and notes receivable transactions

1.

GENERAL JOURNAL

PAGE 3

DATE	ACCOUNT TITLE	DOC. NO.	POST. REF.	DEBIT	CREDIT	
						1
						2
						3
						4
						5
						6
						7
						8
						9
						10

2.

CASH RECEIPTS JOURNAL

PAGE 6

				1 GENERAL	2 GENERAL	3 ACCOUNTS RECEIVABLE	4 SALES	5 SALES TAX PAYABLE	6 SALES TAX PAYABLE	7 SALES DISCOUNT	8 CASH	
DATE	ACCOUNT TITLE	DOC. NO.	POST. REF.	DEBIT	CREDIT	CREDIT	CREDIT	DEBIT	CREDIT	DEBIT	DEBIT	
												1
												2
												3
												4
												5
												6
												7
												8

CASH PAYMENTS JOURNAL

PAGE 10

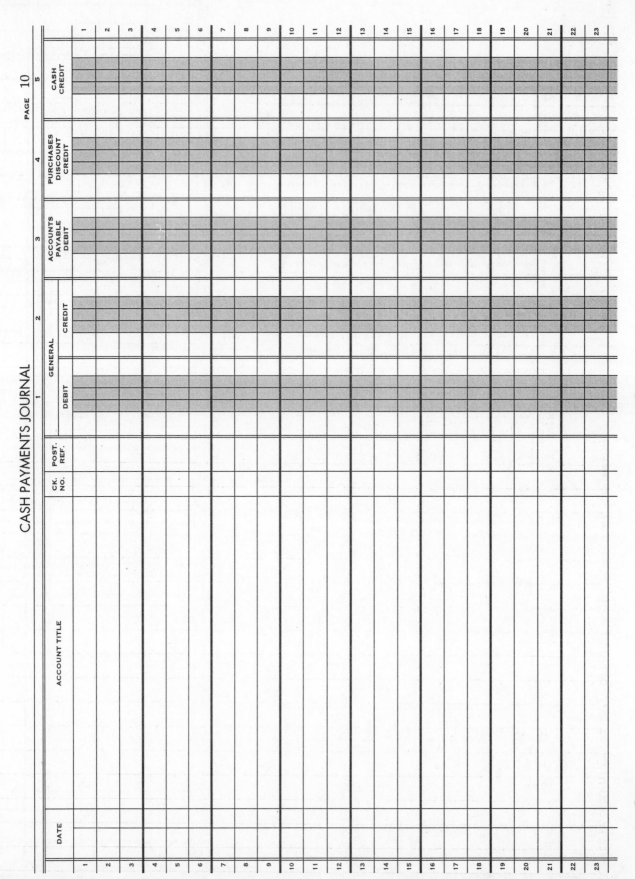

DATE	ACCOUNT TITLE	CK. NO.	POST. REF.	GENERAL DEBIT	GENERAL CREDIT	ACCOUNTS PAYABLE DEBIT	PURCHASES DISCOUNT CREDIT	CASH CREDIT
				1	2	3	4	5

23-1 **RECYCLING PROBLEM** (concluded)

2.

Extra form

24-1 RECYCLING PROBLEM, p. C-24

Journalizing and posting entries for accrued interest revenue and expense

1.

Rucker Company

Work Sheet

For Year Ended December 31, 20X1

			1		2		3		4	
	ACCOUNT TITLE		TRIAL BALANCE				ADJUSTMENTS			
			DEBIT		CREDIT		DEBIT		CREDIT	
4	Interest Receivable									
15	Interest Payable									
50	Interest Income				1 8 9 7 00					
51	Interest Expense		2 4 5 8 00							

2., 3.

GENERAL JOURNAL   PAGE 15

	DATE	ACCOUNT TITLE	DOC. NO.	POST. REF.	DEBIT	CREDIT	
1							1
2							2
3							3
4							4
5							5
6							6
7							7
8							8
9							9
10							10
11							11

4.

GENERAL JOURNAL   PAGE 16

	DATE	ACCOUNT TITLE	DOC. NO.	POST. REF.	DEBIT	CREDIT	
1							1
2							2
3							3
4							4
5							5

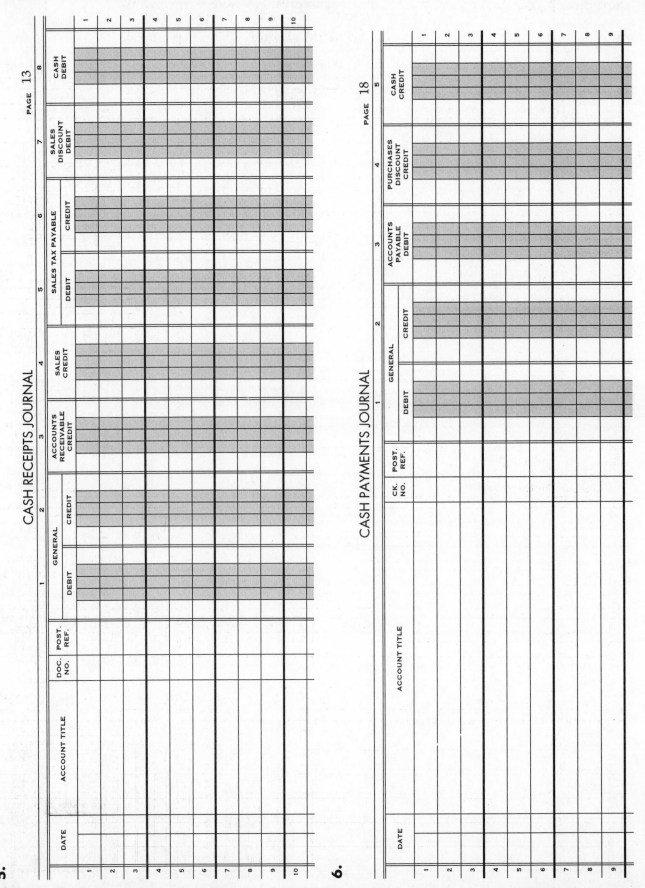

5.

CASH RECEIPTS JOURNAL

PAGE 13

6.

CASH PAYMENTS JOURNAL

PAGE 18

24-1 RECYCLING PROBLEM (continued)

2., 3., 4., 5., 6.

GENERAL LEDGER

ACCOUNT **Notes Receivable**   ACCOUNT NO. 1115

DATE	ITEM	POST. REF.	DEBIT	CREDIT	BALANCE DEBIT	BALANCE CREDIT
Nov. 9		G14	8 0 0 00		8 0 0 00	

ACCOUNT **Interest Receivable**   ACCOUNT NO. 1120

DATE	ITEM	POST. REF.	DEBIT	CREDIT	BALANCE DEBIT	BALANCE CREDIT

ACCOUNT **Notes Payable**   ACCOUNT NO. 2105

DATE	ITEM	POST. REF.	DEBIT	CREDIT	BALANCE DEBIT	BALANCE CREDIT
Dec. 14		CR12		4 8 0 0 00		4 8 0 0 00

ACCOUNT **Interest Payable**   ACCOUNT NO. 2110

DATE	ITEM	POST. REF.	DEBIT	CREDIT	BALANCE DEBIT	BALANCE CREDIT

2., 3., 4., 5., 6.

GENERAL LEDGER

ACCOUNT Income Summary   ACCOUNT NO. 3120

DATE	ITEM	POST. REF.	DEBIT	CREDIT	BALANCE DEBIT	BALANCE CREDIT

ACCOUNT Interest Income   ACCOUNT NO. 7110

DATE	ITEM	POST. REF.	DEBIT	CREDIT	BALANCE DEBIT	BALANCE CREDIT
Dec. 31		CR12		8 5 00		1 8 9 7 00

ACCOUNT Interest Expense   ACCOUNT NO. 8105

DATE	ITEM	POST. REF.	DEBIT	CREDIT	BALANCE DEBIT	BALANCE CREDIT
Dec. 31		CP12	1 0 0 00		2 4 5 8 00	

25-1 RECYCLING PROBLEM, p. C-25

Journalizing dividends and preparing a work sheet for a corporation

1.

GENERAL JOURNAL

PAGE 12

DATE	ACCOUNT TITLE	DOC. NO.	POST. REF.	DEBIT	CREDIT

2.

CASH PAYMENTS JOURNAL

PAGE 18

DATE	ACCOUNT TITLE	CK. NO.	POST. REF.	GENERAL DEBIT	GENERAL CREDIT	ACCOUNTS PAYABLE DEBIT	PURCHASES DISCOUNT CREDIT	CASH CREDIT

3., 4., 6.

Dugan Corporation

Work Sheet

For Year Ended December 31, 20- -

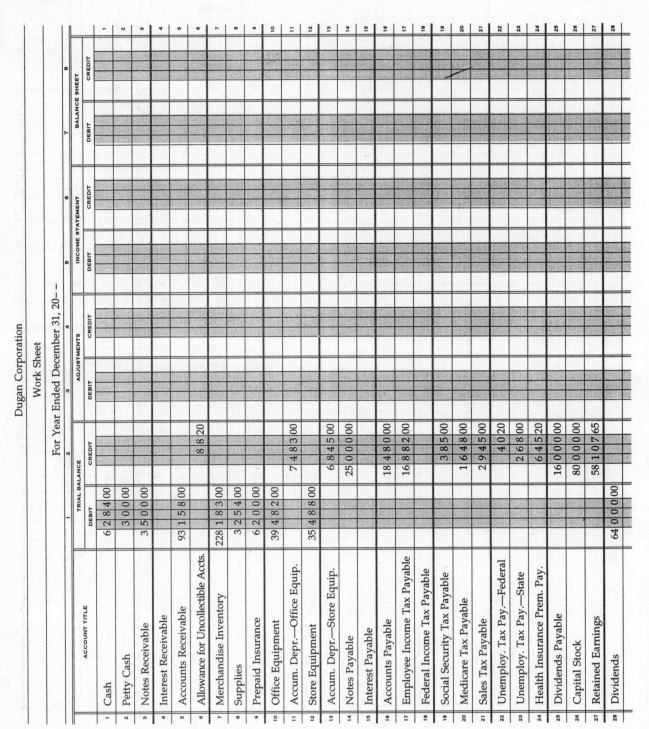

	ACCOUNT TITLE	TRIAL BALANCE DEBIT	TRIAL BALANCE CREDIT	ADJUSTMENTS DEBIT	ADJUSTMENTS CREDIT	INCOME STATEMENT DEBIT	INCOME STATEMENT CREDIT	BALANCE SHEET DEBIT	BALANCE SHEET CREDIT
1	Cash	6 2 8 4 00							
2	Petty Cash	3 0 0 00							
3	Notes Receivable	3 5 0 0 00							
4	Interest Receivable								
5	Accounts Receivable	93 1 5 8 00							
6	Allowance for Uncollectible Accts.		8 8 20						
7	Merchandise Inventory	228 1 8 3 00							
8	Supplies	3 2 5 4 00							
9	Prepaid Insurance	6 2 0 0 00							
10	Office Equipment	39 4 8 2 00							
11	Accum. Depr.—Office Equip.		7 4 8 3 00						
12	Store Equipment	35 4 8 8 00							
13	Accum. Depr.—Store Equip.		6 8 4 5 00						
14	Notes Payable		25 0 0 0 00						
15	Interest Payable								
16	Accounts Payable		18 4 8 0 00						
17	Employee Income Tax Payable		16 8 8 2 00						
18	Federal Income Tax Payable								
19	Social Security Tax Payable		3 8 5 00						
20	Medicare Tax Payable		1 6 4 8 00						
21	Sales Tax Payable		2 9 4 5 00						
22	Unemploy. Tax Pay.—Federal		4 0 20						
23	Unemploy. Tax Pay.—State		2 6 8 00						
24	Health Insurance Prem. Pay.		6 4 5 20						
25	Dividends Payable		16 0 0 0 00						
26	Capital Stock		80 0 0 0 00						
27	Retained Earnings		58 1 0 7 65						
28	Dividends	64 0 0 0 00							

25-1 RECYCLING PROBLEM (concluded)

3., 4., 6.

Dugan Corporation

Work Sheet (continued)

For Year Ended December 31, 20– –

	ACCOUNT TITLE	TRIAL BALANCE DEBIT	TRIAL BALANCE CREDIT	ADJUSTMENTS DEBIT	ADJUSTMENTS CREDIT	INCOME STATEMENT DEBIT	INCOME STATEMENT CREDIT	BALANCE SHEET DEBIT	BALANCE SHEET CREDIT
29	Income Summary								
30	Sales		1684 2 8 4 00						
31	Sales Discount	3 4 1 5 00							
32	Sales Returns and Allow.	6 1 3 5 00							
33	Purchases	1051 1 1 8 00							
34	Purchases Discount		7 8 4 1 00						
35	Purchases Returns and Allow.		13 9 5 8 00						
36	Advertising Expense	36 4 8 3 00							
37	Cash Short and Over	4 25							
38	Credit Card Fee Expense	10 2 5 8 00							
39	Depr. Expense—Office Equip.								
40	Depr. Expense—Store Equip.								
41	Insurance Expense								
42	Miscellaneous Expense	16 4 8 3 00							
43	Payroll Taxes Expense	14 2 4 8 00							
44	Rent Expense	28 0 0 0 00							
45	Repair Expense	4 2 1 8 00							
46	Salary Expense	178 4 1 8 00							
47	Supplies Expense								
48	Uncollectible Accounts Exp.								
49	Utilities Expense	10 1 5 8 00							
50	Gain on Plant Assets		7 4 8 00						
51	Interest Income		6 4 8 00						
52	Interest Expense	3 2 5 1 00							
53	Loss on Plant Assets	2 5 8 00							
54	Federal Income Tax Exp.	100 0 0 0 00							
55		1942 2 9 6 25	1942 2 9 6 25						
56	Net Income after Fed. Inc. Tax								
57									

5. Total of Income Statement Credit column _____

Less total of Income Statement Debit column

before federal income tax _____

Equals Net Income before Federal Income Tax ═══════════════

Extra form

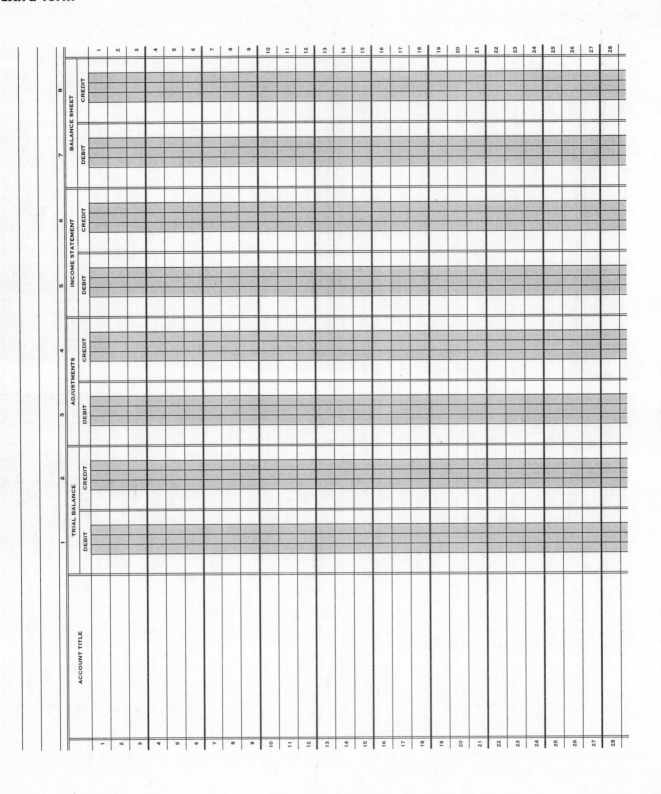

26-1 RECYCLING PROBLEM, p. C-26

Preparing financial statements and end-of-fiscal-period entries for a corporation

Dugan Corporation

Work Sheet

For Year Ended December 31, 20— —

#	ACCOUNT TITLE	Trial Balance Debit	Trial Balance Credit	Adjustments Debit	Adjustments Credit	Income Statement Debit	Income Statement Credit	Balance Sheet Debit	Balance Sheet Credit
1	Cash	6 2 8 4 00						6 2 8 4 00	
2	Petty Cash	3 0 0 00						3 0 0 00	
3	Notes Receivable	3 5 0 0 00						3 5 0 0 00	
4	Interest Receivable			(a) 6 0 00				6 0 00	
5	Accounts Receivable	93 1 5 8 00						93 1 5 8 00	
6	Allowance for Uncollectible Accts.		8 8 20		(b) 8 8 0 00				8 8 8 20
7	Merchandise Inventory	228 1 8 3 00			(c) 20 6 0 0 00			207 5 8 3 00	
8	Supplies	3 2 5 4 00			(d) 1 8 0 0 00			1 4 5 4 00	
9	Prepaid Insurance	6 2 0 0 00			(e) 2 0 0 00			4 2 0 0 00	
10	Office Equipment	39 4 8 2 00						39 4 8 2 00	
11	Accum. Depr.—Office Equip.		7 4 8 3 00		(f) 4 3 0 0 00				11 7 8 3 00
12	Store Equipment	35 4 8 8 00						35 4 8 8 00	
13	Accum. Depr.—Store Equip.		6 8 4 5 00		(g) 5 2 0 0 00				12 0 4 5 00
14	Notes Payable		25 0 0 0 00						25 0 0 0 00
15	Interest Payable				(h) 5 0 00				5 0 00
16	Accounts Payable		18 4 8 0 00						18 4 8 0 00
17	Employee Income Tax Pay.		16 8 8 2 00						16 8 8 2 00
18	Federal Income Tax Payable				(i) 9 8 7 78				9 8 7 78
19	Social Security Tax Payable		3 8 5 00						3 8 5 00
20	Medicare Tax Payable		1 6 4 8 00						1 6 4 8 00
21	Sales Tax Payable		2 9 4 5 00						2 9 4 5 00
22	Unemploy. Tax Pay.—Federal		4 0 20						4 0 20
23	Unemploy. Tax Pay.—State		2 6 8 00						2 6 8 00
24	Health Insurance Prem. Pay.		6 4 5 20						6 4 5 20
25	Dividends Payable		16 0 0 0 00						16 0 0 0 00
26	Capital Stock		80 0 0 0 00						80 0 0 0 00
27	Retained Earnings		58 1 0 7 65						58 1 0 7 65
28	Dividends	64 0 0 0 00						64 0 0 0 00	

Dugan Corporation

Work Sheet (continued)

For Year Ended December 31, 20--

	ACCOUNT TITLE	TRIAL BALANCE DEBIT	TRIAL BALANCE CREDIT	ADJUSTMENTS DEBIT	ADJUSTMENTS CREDIT	INCOME STATEMENT DEBIT	INCOME STATEMENT CREDIT	BALANCE SHEET DEBIT	BALANCE SHEET CREDIT	
29	Income Summary			(c) 20 6 0 0 00		20 6 0 0 00				29
30	Sales		1484 2 8 4 00				1484 2 8 4 00			30
31	Sales Discount	3 4 1 5 00				3 4 1 5 00				31
32	Sales Returns and Allow.	6 1 3 5 00				6 1 3 5 00				32
33	Purchases	851 1 1 8 00				851 1 1 8 00				33
34	Purchases Discount		7 8 4 1 00				7 8 4 1 00			34
35	Purchases Returns and Allow.		13 9 5 8 00				13 9 5 8 00			35
36	Advertising Expense	36 4 8 3 00				36 4 8 3 00				36
37	Cash Short and Over	4 25				4 25				37
38	Credit Card Fee Expense	10 2 5 8 00				10 2 5 8 00				38
39	Depr. Expense—Office Equip.			(f) 4 3 0 0 00		4 3 0 0 00				39
40	Depr. Expense—Store Equip.			(g) 5 2 0 0 00		5 2 0 0 00				40
41	Insurance Expense			(e) 2 0 0 0 00		2 0 0 0 00				41
42	Miscellaneous Expense	16 4 8 3 00				16 4 8 3 00				42
43	Payroll Taxes Expense	14 2 4 8 00				14 2 4 8 00				43
44	Rent Expense	28 0 0 0 00				28 0 0 0 00				44
45	Repair Expense	4 2 1 8 00				4 2 1 8 00				45
46	Salary Expense	178 4 1 8 00				178 4 1 8 00				46
47	Supplies Expense			(d) 1 8 0 0 00		1 8 0 0 00				47
48	Uncollectible Accounts Exp.			(b) 8 8 0 0 00		8 8 0 0 00				48
49	Utilities Expense	10 1 5 8 00				10 1 5 8 00				49
50	Gain on Plant Assets		7 4 8 00				7 4 8 00			50
51	Interest Income		6 4 8 00		(a) 6 0 00		7 0 8 00			51
52	Interest Expense	3 2 5 1 00		(h) 5 0 0 00		3 7 5 1 00				52
53	Loss on Plant Assets	2 5 8 00				2 5 8 00				53
54	Federal Income Tax Exp.	100 0 0 0 00		(i) 9 8 7 78		100 9 8 7 78				54
55		1742 2 9 6 25	1742 2 9 6 25	44 2 4 7 78	44 2 4 7 78	1306 6 3 5 03	1507 5 3 9 00	455 5 0 9 00	254 6 0 5 03	55
56	Net Income after Fed. Inc. Tax					200 9 0 3 97			200 9 0 3 97	56
57						1507 5 3 9 00	1507 5 3 9 00	455 5 0 9 00	455 5 0 9 00	57

Extra form

													% OF NET SALES

26-1 **RECYCLING PROBLEM (continued)**

1.

Dugan Corporation

Income Statement

For Year Ended December 31, 20– –

		% OF NET SALES

26-1 RECYCLING PROBLEM (continued)

1.

Dugan Corporation

Income Statement (continued)

For Year Ended December 31, 20– –

					% OF NET SALES

3.

Dugan Corporation

Statement of Stockholders' Equity

For Year Ended December 31, 20– –

4.

Dugan Corporation

Balance Sheet

December 31, 20– –

26-1 RECYCLING PROBLEM (continued)

4.

Dugan Corporation

Balance Sheet (continued)

December 31, 20– –

2.

Income Statement Analysis

	Acceptable %	Actual %	Positive Result		Recommended Action if Needed
			Yes	No	
Cost of merchandise sold	Not more than 64.0%				
Gross profit on operations	Not less than 36.0%				
Total operating expenses	Not more than 20.0%				
Income from operations	Not less than 16.0%				
Net deduction from other revenue and expenses	Not more than 1.0%				
Net income before federal income tax	Not less than 15.0%				

5.

Balance Sheet Analysis

	Acceptable	Actual	Positive Result		Recommended Action if Needed
			Yes	No	
Working capital	Not less than $200,000.00				
Current ratio	Between 3.0 to 1 and 4.0 to 1				

6.

	GENERAL JOURNAL		PAGE 15	

	DATE	ACCOUNT TITLE	DOC. NO.	POST. REF.	DEBIT	CREDIT	
1							1
2							2
3							3
4							4
5							5
6							6
7							7
8							8
9							9
10							10
11							11
12							12
13							13
14							14
15							15
16							16
17							17
18							18
19							19
20							20
21							21
22							22
23							23
24							24
25							25
26							26
27							27
28							28
29							29
30							30
31							31
32							32
33							33

26-1 RECYCLING PROBLEM (continued)

7.

GENERAL JOURNAL

	DATE	ACCOUNT TITLE	DOC. NO.	POST. REF.	DEBIT	CREDIT	
1							1
2							2
3							3
4							4
5							5
6							6
7							7
8							8
9							9
10							10
11							11
12							12
13							13
14							14
15							15
16							16
17							17
18							18
19							19
20							20
21							21
22							22
23							23
24							24
25							25
26							26
27							27
28							28
29							29
30							30
31							31
32							32
33							33

8.

GENERAL JOURNAL   PAGE 17

DATE	ACCOUNT TITLE	DOC. NO.	POST. REF.	DEBIT	CREDIT	
1						1
2						2
3						3
4						4
5						5
6						6
7						7
8						8
9						9
10						10
11						11
12						12
13						13
14						14
15						15
16						16
17						17
18						18
19						19
20						20
21						21
22						22
23						23
24						24
25						25
26						26
27						27
28						28
29						29
30						30
31						31
32						32
33						33

Extra form

Extra form

Extra form

JOURNAL

		1	2	3	4	5	6	7	8	9	10	11	12	13	14	15	16	17	18	19	20	21	22	23	24	25

Extra form

JOURNAL

					GENERAL		SALES	CASH				
DATE	ACCOUNT TITLE	DOC. NO.	POST. REF.	DEBIT	CREDIT	CREDIT	DEBIT	CREDIT				
				1	2	3	4	5	PAGE			

Name _____ Date _____ Class _____

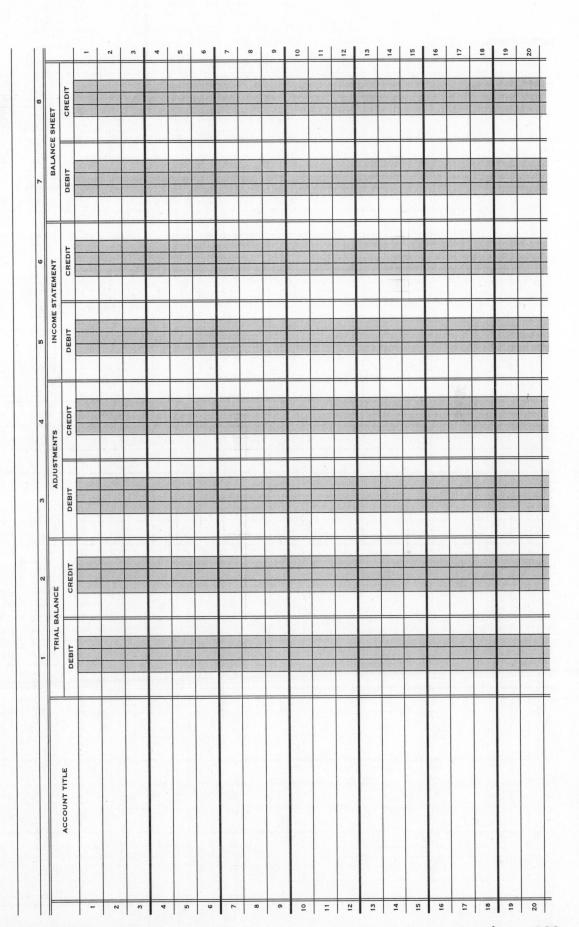

Extra form

Extra form

JOURNAL

	DATE		ACCOUNT TITLE	DOC. NO.	POST. REF.	GENERAL 1 DEBIT	GENERAL 2 CREDIT	ACCOUNTS RECEIVABLE 3 DEBIT	ACCOUNTS RECEIVABLE 4 CREDIT	
1										1
2										2
3										3
4										4
5										5
6										6
7										7
8										8
9										9
10										10
11										11
12										12
13										13
14										14
15										15
16										16
17										17
18										18
19										19
20										20
21										21
22										22
23										23
24										24
25										25
26										26
27										27
28										28
29										29
30										30
31										31
32										32
33										33

Extra form

PAGE

	5	6	7	8	9	10	11	
	SALES CREDIT	SALES TAX PAYABLE CREDIT	ACCOUNTS PAYABLE		PURCHASES DEBIT	CASH		
			DEBIT	CREDIT		DEBIT	CREDIT	
1								1
2								2
3								3
4								4
5								5
6								6
7								7
8								8
9								9
10								10
11								11
12								12
13								13
14								14
15								15
16								16
17								17
18								18
19								19
20								20
21								21
22								22
23								23
24								24
25								25
26								26
27								27
28								28
29								29
30								30
31								31
32								32
33								33

Extra form

				% OF SALES

Extra form

Extra form

Extra forms

GENERAL LEDGER

ACCOUNT _____ ACCOUNT NO. _____

DATE		ITEM	POST. REF.	DEBIT	CREDIT	BALANCE	
						DEBIT	CREDIT

ACCOUNT _____ ACCOUNT NO. _____

DATE		ITEM	POST. REF.	DEBIT	CREDIT	BALANCE	
						DEBIT	CREDIT

ACCOUNT _____ ACCOUNT NO. _____

DATE		ITEM	POST. REF.	DEBIT	CREDIT	BALANCE	
						DEBIT	CREDIT

ACCOUNT _____ ACCOUNT NO. _____

DATE		ITEM	POST. REF.	DEBIT	CREDIT	BALANCE	
						DEBIT	CREDIT

ACCOUNTS PAYABLE LEDGER

VENDOR _____   VENDOR NO. _____

DATE	ITEM	POST. REF.	DEBIT	CREDIT	CREDIT BALANCE

VENDOR _____   VENDOR NO. _____

DATE	ITEM	POST. REF.	DEBIT	CREDIT	CREDIT BALANCE

VENDOR _____   VENDOR NO. _____

DATE	ITEM	POST. REF.	DEBIT	CREDIT	CREDIT BALANCE

VENDOR _____   VENDOR NO. _____

DATE	ITEM	POST. REF.	DEBIT	CREDIT	CREDIT BALANCE

Extra forms

ACCOUNTS RECEIVABLE LEDGER

CUSTOMER _____ CUSTOMER NO. _____

DATE	ITEM	POST. REF.	DEBIT	CREDIT	DEBIT BALANCE

CUSTOMER _____ CUSTOMER NO. _____

DATE	ITEM	POST. REF.	DEBIT	CREDIT	DEBIT BALANCE

CUSTOMER _____ CUSTOMER NO. _____

DATE	ITEM	POST. REF.	DEBIT	CREDIT	DEBIT BALANCE

CUSTOMER _____ CUSTOMER NO. _____

DATE	ITEM	POST. REF.	DEBIT	CREDIT	DEBIT BALANCE

Extra form

	DATE		ACCOUNT TITLE	DOC. NO.	POST. REF.	DEBIT	CREDIT	
1								1
2								2
3								3
4								4
5								5
6								6
7								7
8								8
9								9
10								10
11								11
12								12
13								13
14								14
15								15
16								16
17								17
18								18
19								19
20								20
21								21
22								22
23								23
24								24
25								25
26								26
27								27
28								28
29								29
30								30
31								31
32								32
33								33